THE
SEARCH
for *Peace*

THE
SEARCH
for *Peace*

A Women's GUIDE
to
SPIRITUAL WHOLENESS

Wanda Winters-Gutierrez

Destiny Image₀ Publishers, Inc.
P.O. Box 310
Shippensburg, PA 17257-0310

"Speaking to the Purposes of God for This Generation
and for the Generations to Come"

ISBN 0-7684-2967-6

For Worldwide Distribution
Printed in the U.S.A.

This book and all other Destiny Image, Revival Press, MercyPlace,
Fresh Bread, Destiny Image Fiction, and Treasure House books are
available at Christian bookstores and distributors worldwide.

1 2 3 4 5 6 7 8 9 10 / 09 08 07 06 05 04

For a U.S. bookstore nearest you, call
1-800-722-6774.

For more information on foreign distributors, call
717-532-3040.

Or reach us on the Internet:
www.destinyimage.com

Dedication

To my husband, my beloved…

who builds foundations under dreams and visions. Without the peace and protective love you wrap around me daily, this book would never have been written.

To all my daughters…

Lisa and Sherry, who by their births made me a mom and by their lives make me proud.

Jeni and Nicole, who were God's gifts to my sons and the answers to years of prayers.

Pam, Stacy, Debbie, and Elizabeth, blessings to my soul and forever living in my heart.

And above all, to Father…

Thank You, "Papa," for entrusting me with the "golden dream" of bringing your daughters back home to Your heart.

Acknowledgments

WITH THANKS AND APPRECIATION

Years ago when my soul was first emerging from a long cold night, still wounded from a lifetime of unhealed hurts and full of unresolved issues, I moved to El Paso, Texas. I came with my 30-something daughter Sherry, who was also seeking a new beginning. Even though we were "walking wounded" refugees from "the church," we loved God and wanted to worship Him. In my typical, take-no-hostages (at any time) style, I delivered this ultimatum: "Okay Sher, we'll go to church…but let me tell you, Girl, I'm going late and I'm going to leave early. I don't want to know anybody…and I will never again get involved in any kind of ministry." I leveled her with my most piercing gaze and finished with, "Do you understand me?" She grinned and said, "Yeah, I hear you…but I got to tell you, Mom, I had a dream and saw you sitting at a table teaching women." My lightning response was, "That wasn't a dream, dear…that was a nightmare."

A year later I found myself sitting at a table, in a church fellowship hall, surrounded by women. I still don't know how it happened. I had no idea what to teach, so I just shared my own sad, pitiful story. Then I shared T.D. Jakes' classic healing book, *Woman, Thou Art Loosed!* All we did was face our past and tried to follow the Bishop as he took us step-by-step into wholeness. (Thank you, Bishop Jakes.) They were a brave group of women who first gathered around a wounded leader when "Women of Peace" began. And out of that ministry came this book.

Thank you, blessings, and gracias to the original "Women of Peace"…Sherry, for dreaming the dream; Raphaela, Rhonda, Terry, Virginia, Veronica, Celia, Harriet, Yoli; and, to Bonnie who prophetically gave us our name, "Women of Peace," before I even knew what "peace" was.

Thanks to Pastor Tom Brown who first gave us a place to meet and for opening his pulpit at Word of Life for me to share the vision so many years ago. To Pastors Art and Virginia Soliz, for continually spreading the word about "Women of Peace" and sending so many ladies our way. To precious friends, Don and Rhonda Newbury, who read and prayed over and blessed this material from the beginning.

Thanks especially to the "Women of Peace" who now circle me daily in love and affirmation. Connie, Terry, Gracie, Gigi, Rhonda, Teresa, Ester, Ashleigh, Maggie, Sylvia, Raquel, Melissa, Sarah, Araceli, Sherry, Lisa, Grace, Beth, Gloria, and Lynette. You were among the first to embrace and nurture this material, making it your own by praying, sharing, reading, studying, completing the assignments, making copies, and sending them across the country…spreading the *peace*.

I owe the most profound debt of gratitude to my right-hand enabler, best girlfriend Connie Bustos. As a world-class intercessor you prayed, believed, and were an ever-present sounding board to this ministry. Thank you for taking over my duties at the ministry center while this book was being fine-tuned. You are indeed a gift from Father to me.

I would like to acknowledge my four children, Lisa, Sherry, Mike, and Chris and their mates. Each of you in your unique way have been instrumental in the final version of this project. Each of you are a joy to my soul and fill my heart with pride. Thanks for always being there for me, even as I traveled the sometimes turbulent waters of my journey. Your lives continually inspire me to higher heights.

Thanks to two good friends, Rev. M.V. and Pastor D.C. You put up with a lot of my "unresolved issues" and through your forgiveness helped me take this journey home to Father's heart.

Once again, gracias to my beloved Hector. Your faith in the call of God upon my life and your never-ending generosity, thoughtfulness, wit, wisdom, guidance, and love has freed me to follow my destiny.

Acknowledgments

Grateful acknowledgments must go to Don Milam, vice president of acquisitions, and the entire staff at Destiny Image. Special thanks to Lisa Ott for her vital touches, you are much appreciated. Blessings to editor-extraordinaire Becky Helman whose anointed presence gave this project needed structure and taught me the value of lower case letters. Thank you all for being sensitive to the Spirit and to a novice author. Needless to say without your creative, Spirit-led expertise, this final product would not have been the same. The lives this book will impact have you to thank for catching the vision and making it a reality.

Endorsements

Once in a while we get an epiphany, one more piece of the puzzle on our way to becoming whole. *The Search for Peace* is such an experience. As a Holocaust survivor and a lost child of the 60's, controlled by the insidious manipulator Charles Manson, I had many unresolved issues. And I am convinced this book was written especially for me—you will feel the same. You will want all the people you care about to read it. But don't give up your copy. Read it and read it well...then read it again. You will never be the same.

Catherine Share
Musician, Author, Minister

"The lady who writes so beautifully,"—that was my description of Wanda. I "happened" into a meeting when she was reading from one of her journals...I know it was a divine connection. I have learned so much from her and especially from the material in this book. *The Search for Peace* challenges us to journey into the realms of our soul and leave behind our old nature to become great Women of Peace. I love this book. It has helped me to let go of the past, live in the present, and pursue the future in the Presence. I know the spirit of the woman behind this book...she is my friend, prayer partner, and teacher...she is definitely a woman after God's own heart.

Connie Bustos
Founder, It's All About Jesus Ministries

As I read, I journeyed with Wanda. I could tell she had passed this way before. She leads with experience, reaches out with compassion, and pauses with concern to recall for us the way she found Peace. Take the journey, for God has placed in our midst those who can instruct, encourage, and inspire; and Wanda is one of those.

Lynette Lepinski
Minister, Song Writer,
Recording Artist

From the very first moment I met Wanda, I immediately knew she had something special. I didn't know what it was, but there was a sense of comfort I felt around her. I don't know how to explain it, but she radiates Peace…a peace that makes people feel at ease, and makes you want to know what she knows. Her ministry has changed my life. Because of her ministry and example of love, my family has begun a journey here on earth that has moved us into the Kingdom of God…the Kingdom of Peace. This book will do the same for you.

Gigi Silerio
Woman of Peace

The Search for Peace is a unique book for this hour. It captures God's heart to bring healing and wholeness in women's lives. In the battle of the soul, Wanda gives insights that will enable God's daughters to fulfill their destiny and live an overcoming life.

Rev. James W. Nunes
Pastor and International Minister

Table of Contents

A Word Before the Journey

The reason for this book began in the *heart of God* during the eternities past. For every one of His *beloved daughters*, Father had a dream—a dream full of endless possibilities, honor, and *peace*. That *golden dream in the heart of God* for us is still attainable. The barrier that holds us back is our being unable to understand who the enemy is, and how we have opened the door to the dream thief. That and the fact that we have settled for less…far too long.

We were born to be *princesses in the realm of glory*. We were born to be part of the *glorious endtime Church,* walking upon the earth with signs and wonders following. We were created special for this place in time…and it's past time we began to act like who we say we are…*daughters of Almighty God* and heirs in the *Kingdom of Peace.* Our crown has been paid for by the blood of Jesus. We need to place it on our heads and wear it proudly.

Peace in the original language of the Bible means, among other things, "nothing missing and nothing broken." As a long-time member of the Body of Christ, I have never had to look very far in the Church to find broken and missing pieces, which equates to a lack of *peace*. As a wise man said, "These things ought not to be." I believe that before the return of Christ these things will cease to be. Father has a *grand dream* for His children who hunger and thirst for peace.

A snapshot of His *dream* can be found in **First Thessalonians 5:23-24:**

*And may the God of peace Himself sanctify you through and through [separate you from profane things, make you pure and wholly consecrated to God]; and may your **spirit** and **soul** and **body** be preserved sound and complete [and found] blameless at the coming of our Lord Jesus Christ[the Messiah]. Faithful is He Who is calling you [to Himself] and utterly trustworthy, and He will also do it [fulfill His call by hallowing and keeping you].)*

Paraphrased *Up Close and Personal* that Scripture says, "That the *God of nothing missing and nothing broken* (our Father), wants us to be *whole* in our spirits and souls and bodies when Christ comes back. Not only that, He Himself is utterly trustworthy to fulfill His own *call* by helping us accomplish that very thing."

That is why this book was written—to help move us from broken and missing to *wholeness* and *peace*, to move us from emptiness to *fullness*, to move us out of death into *destiny*.

The choice is ours. Only ours. We do not need anyone's permission. We can stay where we are or implement the changes that will take us where we ought to be—living in the *heart dream of God*, no longer dying before we are fully born.

Questions and Undreamed-of Devastations

I hear it all the time...

"I need help...I want to live a victorious Christian life, but no matter how hard I try, I keep drowning in my own failures."

"I don't know what God wants me to do; sometimes I think I know, but I have been wrong so many times I'm almost tired of trying."

"There are unanswered questions in my heart, and I simply cannot figure out why devastating things keep happening in my life and for that matter in the church."

"I do everything I know to do. I tithe, confess the Word, repent, forgive others, pray, and still my basic prayers go unanswered. What am I doing wrong?"

These questions usually come from Christian women who have been in the church for years. They are valid concerns.

Unfortunately, it is a sadly common occurrence in all social and economic levels and in every type of congregation from mainline to independent charismatic. God's people, born again, His Spirit residing within them, are still experiencing one failure after another, one disappointment after another. Where do we go to for help when there are even spiritual leaders who are deceived and end up doing unthinkable

17

things bringing devastation upon their families, their ministries, and causing confusion in the Body of Christ?

A pastor will leave his wife and family searching for fulfillment in the arms of another woman, leaving a wounded mother to answer her child's, "Where did Daddy go?" and a congregation asking basically the same question.

A woman minister, struggling with rejection from her husband, heard a voice saying, "The thinner you are the more he will want you," and began a 10-year battle with bulimia, damaging her body and her self-esteem. No matter how thin she became he never wanted her; yet she was fully convinced the voice was God's.

A teen, raised in a Christian home, attending church regularly, writes a note of heartbreaking emptiness, right before she takes her own life.

A beloved and effective children's pastor is found to be a pedophile, but only after causing years of trauma in the lives of the innocent.

A beautiful Christian woman stays in an abusive situation with an alcoholic husband. For more than 20 years they haven't had a marriage. She's depressed, lonely, tired, and confused. She is a long-time member of the largest and most effective church in her city and sings in the choir, yet lives a secret life of torment.

A pastor's wife is deceived into thinking a soft-spoken deacon is God's gift to her lonely, unfulfilled life, plunging herself and her family into years of hell on earth.

A lovely young mother, a strong leader in her church and community—the kind of person people look up to, a role model trusted beyond question. A few hours before she and her family go to church to celebrate Mother's Day, she kills two of her children and leaves her fourteen-month-old baby bleeding and near death in his crib. She says she had a vision and God told her to do it. Stunned and shocked, her pastor stands and weeps. His sister-in-law is in jail; two of his nephews are dead; the third is in critical condition; and, nobody saw it coming.

I wish these were isolated incidents. I wish these kinds of things happened only in Hollywood movies and not in my town and yours...not in my church and yours...not in my life and yours.

How is it that people can be deceived into justifying such acts? Why is it that God's people cannot see with eyes that see and hear with ears that hear? Why can we not tap into the wonders of God's grace and live there? Why does the Christian life seem like one endless battle after another for some of us? Where does satan get in?

More Questions

Then there are the other questions that won't go away—perhaps not as earth shattering until we realize that the answers to these questions might have prevented the unthinkable things that tear out our hearts.

Questions such as:

How can I move beyond the pain of past mistakes and failure to live a peaceful life?

What is *peace* anyway?

How can I set boundaries in my life so I am not taken advantage of and abused?

I am a Christian...why do I get depressed?

Isn't there more to life than work, bills, and worry?

Why is it that no matter how successful I am, I still feel empty?

What am I here for?

How does one know the voice of God?

Does God have a specific plan for my life?

Does He even know my name?

There must be answers. A way of wholeness, a way to live that gives satan no place. Surely God has a better dream than what we have experienced for most of our Christian lives. All around the world I hear the same cry coming from the hearts of the women of God, "There must be *more*! I am a mess and my family is a mess!" None of these things can be in the *plan of God* for His children. We are called to a higher life, and it must be attainable. But how...where...and dear God...when?

For over half a century I have stumbled around the never-never land of almost being there. For too many years of being a Christian, I simply could not lay hold of the *peace* that I knew to be mine in Christ Jesus. I feel I have traveled the uncharted journey that millions of my sisters in the faith are on even now. Fifty-plus years and untold tears later, these things I know for sure.

We have a destination in God's plan; I call it a *Peaceful Kingdom*, where nothing is missing and nothing is broken. In this *Kingdom of Peace* our lives are ruled by the Spirit of God, who is living in our human spirits. When we are able to hear the voice of the Holy Spirit louder and more distinctly than the voices that come through our mind, will, and emotions (otherwise known as our soul), we will be on our way to our *assignment*. We will be on our way to *a place called...peace*. We will be on our way to *days of Heaven on earth*.

Journey to a Peaceful Kingdom

We all have searched
For a Peaceful Kingdom,
A place where all is right
And life has meaning.
We dream endlessly
Into infinity and beyond,
Uselessly…escapes us
Because we have made
The plans not knowing
That Father has "The Plan,"
And it is…His Dream.

Prologue to Part One

DIRECTIONALLY CHALLENGED

This book is designed and written for the *asker of questions,* the *seeker,* and the *pioneer* who is not afraid to discover that *she* may be her own frontier. This book is in your hands not so much to give answers as to create a road map to where answers may be found. As a pastor, teacher, and minister of the gospel of Jesus Christ, I am tired of seeing the daughters of God hurting and in want. I have come to know that our own souls are possibly the "last frontier" we must conquer before we emerge as the *glorious endtime Church* we read about in Scripture. It is time for us to be who we are called to be, part of the literal *Body of Christ* walking upon the earth. This cannot happen until our spirits, souls, and bodies are in perfect alignment to the *golden dream in the heart of God.*

There have been times in my life when I classified myself as "directionally challenged." *North, south, east,* and west are meaningless words to me unless the sun is rising or setting. If it is high noon, I'm lost. I must have instructions that include right and left directives. But I never stay lost long because I'm not afraid to ask questions.

On a road trip by myself, I have been known to ask for directions, drive three miles and ask for directions again. I eventually arrive at my destination. It may take a little time, but I do get there. My children say I make up for lost time with a fast car and wide open Texas highways. (What do children know anyway?)

In my Christian walk I have also been directionally challenged. Some of the questions at the beginning of this book are very much

23

like the ones I have asked over and over again. I desperately needed help, and for more years than I care to admit, I couldn't find anyone who had a map I could understand. I read hundreds of self-help books and took classes about the deeper life. I even taught a few. All of them gave me hope, and I would dutifully write in my journal, "Okay, I am at point A. If I do this, this, and this, I will get to point B and beyond." But I didn't.

There seemed to be a roadblock in my going forward and the roadblock was in me. All the time I appeared, on the surface, to have it together. Success as a wife, mother, minister, and writer of Christian literature, no less! I was in demand as a teacher and special speaker. The articles, poetry, and stories were published in well-known Christian magazines. I had a lot of people fooled a lot of the time. I even had myself fooled part of the time. But I never fooled the Spirit of God who resided in my spirit.

In my more lucid moments I knew I was in trouble. I knew there had to be *more*, to me and for me, but the answers eluded me. There was no lasting peace, no continual success. There had to be more than this void inside me that seemed to absorb all my dreams into its nothingness. Even worse, I was losing my ability to dream.

The Assignment

I knew God had a specific plan for me, but I also knew my very soul was being consumed; and every day I lost a little bit more of the real me (whoever on earth that was). Then satan moved in with his own assignment. He plotted and carefully laid a plan to destroy my life, my ministry, my family. At the time I wasn't aware of what I am about to share with you. I didn't know the difference between my soul, where satan has access, and my spirit where he cannot go.

I heard a voice that said, "Go this way. This is the answer to all your questions...this is the fullness for your emptiness...this is the road." So I went. Not having a map I could understand and true to form, I drove full speed ahead into a brick wall...then I drove off a bridge.

Broken and spiritually bleeding, I finally came to the end of myself. Disoriented, but alive, I looked up and saw Father standing there...both hands reaching for me. In one hand, He held my healing; in the other hand, He held the map to my *assignment*.

The Word of God says, "*You will know the Truth, and the Truth will set you free*" (Jn. 8:32). Sometimes the hardest truth to accept is the truth about oneself. As hard as it may be to swallow, the fact remains—if we don't know what is broken, we will never get it fixed, and our souls are subject to breakage. If you are like me, you know something is not working here, yet you remain clueless. We don't even know how to proceed in our journey to our *personal assignment* from God or even if there is such a thing. Trust me, there is.

Our *assignment* in life is not decided upon, but discovered. I know beyond any and all doubt that each person born has a *purpose* on the earth that only he or she can fulfill. Within this *dream, call, destiny, assignment,* or whatever you choose to call it, lies a life full of meaning and peace. It is our very own *Peaceful Kingdom* where nothing is missing and nothing is broken. It is also within the framework of this *assignment*, we find our own personal *reality and passion*, that which gives us the most joy, completeness, and satisfaction possible.

One of the incredibly remarkable truths about this *assignment* is the fact that when Creator God deposited it in us, He also included every single resource we will ever need to walk it out to the fullest extent, and in the highest possible way. That's what *peace*—nothing missing and nothing broken—means. This *assignment,* as well as the resources to accomplish it, is in our spirits, the eternal part of our beings. Our problem is, we are so well-versed in listening to our mind, will, and emotions (or our souls), that we simply cannot hear the whisper of *the Spirit* in our spirits. It has taken me nearly half a century to get this figured out. God willing, it won't take you that long.

One part of my personal *assignment* is to draw a road map for other women. I am doing this with a sincere desire, revealing honesty and a great deal of faith in the women of God. I believe that if this map has fallen into your hands, God will use it to help create wholeness in you and bring you into a deeper awareness of His perfect *plan* for your life.

I realize it is possible to travel many different roads and end up at the same destination. I also realize that many Christian women are well on their way to their personal *Peaceful Kingdom*. Many more are walking out the *plan of God* for their lives already…for this I praise God.

If you are one of them, please don't discount this map yet. No doubt there are women around you who have yet to hold a map in their hands they can relate to. This may be the very tool they need. Perhaps you can take the *journey* with them. Who knows, you might pick up some travel tips along the way and become a creator of maps yourself.

It Is Never Too Late

Part One of this book deals with the what, when, where, and why we ended up in situations that have so thoroughly derailed us in the past. I believe as you prayerfully read through the first section, you will receive a clear message that there is *more* than you have heretofore experienced. God really and truly knows your name and indeed has a specific plan full of all good things just waiting for you. It is never too late; it is all in your future; and as Mike Murdock says, "God never consults your past when He plans your future."

To be perfectly honest with you, it does not matter right now if you have messed up your own life and everyone else's around you, or if other people have bailed out on you ever since you were born. Nor does it matter whether you are considering checking yourself into a maximum-security facility (can a person do that?), or are just a little off-the-wall now and then.

Nor does it matter if you have only moderately miserable moments or if the misery is like a cancer eating at your soul. What really matters is that you know (or perhaps it is only a hope) that there is *more* and you want with all your heart to find it. That's all that matters. Period. If you seek...you will find. I am living proof.

Part Two is actually the beginning of the *journey*. Through the essays, stories, meditations, disciplines, and assignments, we will receive the light of insight and the power to make quality decisions and sweeping changes. They are the road map into the deepest recesses of our souls. They are signposts pointing to *the assignment*. They are the vehicles that will bring us closer and closer to our destination.

The time and commitment required in this part of the book are absolutely, vitally necessary, and nonnegotiable. It may be the hardest road you have ever traveled. There will be times you will think we are totally offtrack. It may seem like the strangest sort of trip you have ever heard of and you're not even sure you want to go. But hang tough, for we cannot *journey outward* until we *journey inward*.

Inventory of Our Soul

In reality the *journey inward* is taking inventory of our excess baggage, sorting through our souls to see what we need to keep and what will get in the way as we move forward. It is deciding what works for us and what doesn't. Jesus said He is coming for a *glorious Church* without spot or wrinkle. That being the case, something is going to have to change.

Right now, too many in the Body of Christ, underneath the starched and pressed Sunday facade, appear to be rather bruised and dehydrated. It's not that we don't have an abundance of revelation. There are more wonderful books being written; more Word being preached; more prophets, apostles, pastors, and teachers among us than at anytime in the history of man. We simply are not getting it, and we don't know why.

We are the *endtime Church* destined to walk upon this earth as sons and daughters of Almighty God, doing the signs and wonders that Jesus did and more. Before He returns, the world is supposed to look at us in amazement. Our lifestyle and witness will usher in the final harvest of souls. (Well, we do have part of it...they look at us in amazement sometimes, unfortunately not as prophesied.)

But, He *is* coming and we *will* get it, because He has said, *"the Glory of the Lord will cover the earth as the waters cover the sea"* (Isa. 11:9). That *glory* is not going to come down out of the heavens...it is going to come out of us. This tidal wave will come out of the Holy Spirit who is dwelling in our human spirits. The only thing stopping Him is the conditions of our souls. We must make a quality decision to do whatever it takes to *"Prepare in the wilderness the way of the Lord"* (Isa. 40:3).

You are right now, standing halfway between your past and your future. The decision is yours. Before you decide, let me tell you prophetically, that your future shines so bright it hurts my eyes. I see the *women of God* rising out of the ashes of their past and soaring into heights unknown. I see them operating in love and power, fully aware of who they are and what part of *the family business* their Father has placed in their hands. I see them whole and free, and that very freedom and wholeness is bringing new life to everyone around them. That old axiom, "When Mama ain't happy, ain't nobody happy" has a flip side. When a woman is whole...things change.

By design and nature, a woman gives birth to what is inside her. She is a life-giver. The women of God are about to give birth and bring a heretofore, unseen, fresh, and new wholeness to the corporate Body of Christ. Are you ready to step into your part of that vision? Whatever our goal is, we can get there as long as we are honest with ourselves about where we are right now and the work involved in moving forward. There are no back doors, no free rides...just us...this moment and a decision.

No Easy Road

Remember that you have had an up-front fair warning, the *journey inward* is going to be the most difficult and the most necessary part of this adventure. I know this to be the truth because most of us have spent a lifetime and had a lot of help setting up roadblocks, constructing man-made mountains, and diverting raging rivers onto our own paths. Sometimes, the work is so hard, and we get to the place that we wonder if the trip is worth the pain. I can tell you a resounding, YES! Hundreds of other women can tell you the same.

I have taught these principles for years in our *Women of Peace* ministry, one-on-one, on television, and in churches. I often sit in awe as women from all walks of life brake out of the prisons of their wounded souls and walk into a *Peaceful Kingdom*. There no more beautiful words than, *"I am Free! Oh, Father! Thank You! I understand now...and I am free!"* Each time this happens the reality of, *"You shall know the Truth, and the Truth will set you free,"* rings ever new in my heart. We can only add in thanksgiving, *"whom the Son has set free is free indeed!"* (see John 8:36 KJV).

Free From What?

Born into an imperfect world full of imperfect people, few of us get to the age of accountability without having been bruised, wounded, and sidetracked from the unique dream that was in the heart of God when He created us.

Far too many of our heavenly Father's daughters live their whole lives and have no idea how to get out of the cycles of one crisis after another, one failure after another. On the surface, we may appear happy, productive, and very religious. Below the surface, the well is dry and deep. All the time *God's heart dream* for us, the reason we were born, our *assignment* remains buried inside our born-again spirits. A bright, shining, full-of-peace life is waiting to be discovered, excavated, and lived!

So Exactly What Is the Problem Here?

There are a number of problems, but only one source—namely satan, the enemy of our souls. His one passion is to steal, kill, and destroy our *assignments*. Every sad, bad, terrible thing that has ever happened on the earth and in our lives can be traced back to him. Why? It is simple—he is incredibly jealous and afraid of you. *You* are everything he wants to be. Not the *you* we know, but the real *you*. The made-in-the-image-of-God you, the knowing-who-you-are-in-Christ-Jesus and fearlessly-walking-out-the-plan-of-God *you*. That's the *you* he is after.

The adversary wants to keep us blinded, because he knows that when we finally see who our enemy is, the jig is up, and we are about to walk into our *Promised Land*, our personal *Peaceful Kingdom* where he can never steal, kill, or destroy anything ever again.

Someone said, "We have found the enemy and the enemy is us." Yes and no. Satan, pure and simple and unadorned, is our enemy; but somehow he has tricked multiplied millions of us into being our own worst enemies. After a while, we really don't need his evil presence to mess up our lives. We take over for him and sabotage ourselves. We, of course, always give him all the credit.

Yes, we pray, go to church, read the Word. We listen to tapes and go to every laying-on-of-hands meeting that comes to town. And we walk away from that prayer time, church time, Word time, tape time, and laying-on-of-hands time declaring how wonderful it was...but nothing ever changes. We buy anointed books (and some not so anointed), give offerings, get counseling, and call prayer lines. (We would probably dial-a-prophet, if we had a number.) We fast and pray some more and nothing ever, ever changes. Oh well...maybe next time. It's as though we are homesick and can't get home.

After a while it looks like we would catch on—if we want to go some place we have never been, we better do something we have never done, like get a map and get on the right road. Hello us!

The road we have been traveling has very effectively taken us in circles. We have covered the same ground so long we have made a deep rut. It is a very comfortable and religious rut to be sure, lined as it is with our good intentions and sincere hunger for more of God. Besides, we are in good company—most of our friends have a rut just like ours.

It is time for women to get serious about our part of the *golden dream in the heart of God*. Actually it is more serious than we seem to think. Not only are our lives and the lives we are called to impact in jeopardy, but when all is finished and Father folds up this earth like a garment, we want to hear Him say, "WELL DONE, GIRL! You did it! Papa is proud."

God Is in the Details

I believe we have within ourselves the ability to do whatever it takes to get us where we ought to be. Please forgive me as I point out the obvious, that even though a map falls into our hands, it does not automatically mean we have arrived at our destination. We still have to take the trip, travel the road, and pay attention to the signs along the route.

Likewise, simply because we do a quick read of this book does not mean we have "done" the book. If you are like someone else I know (we're not mentioning authors' names here), go ahead and read it through quickly if you must, then go back and "do" the book. Remember, when we fly, we miss a lot of details. Because God is in the details, we can't afford to miss any.

The Search for Peace is designed, to be an adventure guidebook. It can be used in a group or alone. The operative word here is "used." I can absolutely assure you that *if* you follow each week's readings, meditations, and disciplines found in Part Two, at the end of the course you will have more light and revelation on every question in your life. Your relationship with God and everyone around you will be forever changed.

Most importantly you will meet, perhaps for the first time, a remarkably fascinating *lady*, who knows who she is and where she is going. I know that *lady*. She is quietly powerful, sure of herself, and full of *presence*. She moves from a *center* deep within, regardless of what is going on around her.

When she walks into a room, *peace* happens. When she walks into your life, you know things are about to change. Where she walks, people know *royalty* has just set her foot on terra firma. When she touches your soul, healing comes. When she touches your spirit, you fall in love with her King.

This *lady* is the real *you*, walking out your life as Father intended you to walk. You're going to like this *lady*, and you're going to love where she lives...it is called The *Peaceful Kingdom*. In this *Kingdom*, love rules and nothing is missing and nothing is broken.

We are almost ready to begin our *journey*, but first let's find out where all this chaos began.

Part One

God's Journey Outward

In the Beginning…
The Dream in the Heart of God…Plan A

As documented in the Book of Genesis, God said,

*"Let Us [Father, Son, and Holy Spirit] make **mankind** in **our** image, after **our** likeness, and let **them** have complete control and authority over all the works of **our** hands. And so God created man in His **own** image. In the **image** and **likeness** of God created He them.* [Lest someone has a problem about woman being an afterthought and not in the original plan, please note that in the literal Hebrew the above states, "He created Him-Her*both* at the same time, and gave them *both* authority over all the works of His hands.] *And so God made **them** in His exact likeness and breathed into **them** the breath of life. Zoë Life…the God kind of Life. He blessed them and said, "Be fruitful and multiply, fill the earth and subdue it using all its vast resources in serving God and man. Have dominion over everything." And it was so* (paraphrased from the Amplified Bible, *Up Close and Personal*).(The Word *Up Close and Personal* is taking a verse or passage from the Bible and paraphrasing it into your own way of speaking or writing, inserting your name and circumstances into it.)

And God saw everything He had made and behold it was very, very good, suitable, pleasant, and He approved it completely. He created them perfectly. They were just like Him. They were created to live forever. Nowhere in their divine DNA could death be found. God had created His masterpiece, and He crowned them with His glory.

He made a perfect place for them to live. He placed them in the Garden, then He laid down the ground rules. "Okay here's the deal...you may eat freely of everything in the Garden except of the tree of knowledge of good and evil, for in that day you shall surely die." (He was speaking of spiritual death.)

This masterpiece was unlike any other creation God had ever designed. Because He had made them in His exact likeness, they had something in them that nothing else on the earth had...a soul (a mind, a will, and emotions.) Most of the time we define the soul as the element of "free will." That ingredient would enable God's perfect family the ability to make choices. They could choose to obey and serve God...or not. To the angels looking on as all this took place, it must have appeared as if God was taking an extremely risky chance. They were right.

What Was God Thinking?

He was thinking about a family. He was thinking about how much He loved Adam and Eve. He was thinking of all the wonderful times they would have as they worked together running the *family business* (i.e., the whole universe). He was thinking about the fellowship, the walks, the talks. How He must have laughed and enjoyed watching them discover all the wonders He had prepared especially for them. How His Father heart filled with pride when He saw Adam and Eve acting just like Him...speaking things into existence and controlling the world around them with the words of their mouths.

I see Him turning to Gabriel and Michael, His two top angels and saying, "Those kids of Mine...aren't they something!" Imagine the heavenly host looking on and saying (whatever the celestial equivalent of "wow" is), "Wow God, what is man that You have created him and crowned him with Your glory and honor?"

A perfect man, a perfect woman, in a perfect world living 24/7 in the blessings of their Creator Father. That was His *heart dream*. He wanted for all eternity to walk, talk, laugh, and enjoy His family and their descendants. In this perfect world there was no death, no sickness, no fear, no lack. They had everything they needed. If one of them ran short of anything, no problem—all they had to do was open their mouths and speak it into existence. All they knew, they had learned from Papa—and that was how Papa got stuff. Genesis is full of, "And God said...And God said...And God said...and it was so." Adam and Eve were made in His exact likeness, and having been given complete authority over all the earth, no doubt they did the same.

God worked six days, or 6000 years depending on His numerical standard at the time, which quite likely was "a day to Him is as a thousand years" (see 2 Peter 3:8). At any rate, He worked for a specific time upon the earth, trained His children to run the family business, sat down and said, "Okay, there it is. It's yours now. Let's see what you can do with it."

Enter the Decision...Enter Man's Free Will... Enter Fear and Death...Enter Plan B

What Went Wrong?

We have no way of knowing how long this perfect world lasted. It could have been for hundreds of thousands of years, or it could have been three days. In any case, the fact remains that satan found Eden and began to sabotage a perfect world. Adam and Eve, having been created with a free will, sided with him and together a fallen angel and a God-man threw all of creation into chaos.

No longer could God's love-creation walk in unbroken fellowship with Him, Creator and creation moving as one. Adam and Eve's disobedience polluted all of creation right up to, but not including, the throne of God.

Adam had been given a specific time lease upon the earth, which he sublet to satan, and for thousands of earth years the Spirit of God could not relate to His children as He had done with Adam and Eve in the beginning. He was still around, but the intimacy, the oneness, was gone. If He had, as He no doubt wanted to do, put His arms around His fallen son and daughter, His goodness would have destroyed them. Love kept Him away.

God's *heart dream* was still in effect. He wanted to walk and talk with His children. He had a specific *assignment* for each of their lives and the lives of their descendants, you and me. This *assignment* was as wonderfully crafted and detailed as each of His children. The uniqueness of each personal plan would create days of heaven on earth for His kids. Father wanted His family back into the position Adam and Eve were before the fall. The price He had to pay was a dear one…but love is a powerful motivator.

God was so passionately in love with His creation that He had to stay at a distance until Plan B was in place. He began to lay the groundwork for this redemption. He sent prophets, priests, and kings to write the Old Testament. The reoccurring theme was…

I know the thoughts and plans that I have for you…thoughts and plans for welfare and peace and not for evil, to give you hope in your final outcome (Jeremiah 29:11).

The other reoccurring theme was a replay of the message He had delivered to satan's cringing ears in the Garden after the fall:

I am sending One to redeem My Family…He will crush your head…He will bring many Sons back to Glory…He will set the captives free…

Satan's Worst Nightmare

Over the years, that chilling promise continued to bring satan into a state of dread. It was his worst nightmare…that God would send *Someone* to the earth who would be able to reverse the sentence of fear and death he had been holding over human beings. It hounded him day and night. When God told him, *"He will bruise and tread your head underfoot,"* he knew it to be the Truth. As one of the three known archangels, satan had been around God long enough to know that if God said it…it would happen.

The liar had been anointed… had held a high corporate office in God's Kingdom. As a former resident of Heaven, he knew the Boss and he knew the Boss's Son. So from the time God spoke to him in the Garden and on down through the ages, as he heard the same message from prophet after prophet, he began running scared.

Although he knew God was sending a Redeemer, he didn't know when and he didn't know how. So every time he heard that a Deliverer was about to come forth, he tried to kill the seed…he killed the prophets and he continually killed babies. When Moses was about to be born, satan saw to it that babies were murdered. When Jesus was born and the astrologers saw His sign, again satan slaughtered the innocent.

Somehow he would figure out when someone was soon to be born who was destined to shake his kingdom. Have you ever wondered why abortion has hit at an all-time high in our generation? It is quite simple really—he has gotten wind of a generation about to be born who will never quit until he is utterly defeated. This endtime generation will walk in the perfect plan of God for their lives and launch a *shock-and-awe* campaign against him like the world, Heaven, and hell has never seen. If you are reading this, you are part of that chosen generation. If you are reading this, you have escaped being wiped out before your time. If you are reading this, your time is now.

Clueless

When satan failed to kill Jesus as a baby, he continued his search.

One day at the Jordan River, the Spirit of God came upon a young Jewish Rabbi as He was being baptized. So satan followed Him into the wilderness and began his interrogation, trying to find out if He was the Messiah who God had slapped him up side the head with 4,000 years earlier.

He said, "If You are the Son of God…do this and this…." He still wasn't sure if He was the One. So he decided to go ahead and kill Him anyway. Big mistake. Paul writes that if he had known the outcome of the crucifixion, he would never have killed the Lord of glory (I Cor. 2:8). I guess not.

Our enemy in his wildest imagination did not fathom the resurrection. Because *he* held the keys to death, hell, and the grave, he could not conceive of Someone dying, going to hell, taking *his* keys and then raising from the dead. Nor could he comprehend a world full of God-men and God-women knowing themselves to be sons and daughters of Almighty God who held his keys in their own hands. He could not dream your future and mine. Satan puts a whole new dimension to the word "clueless."

You see, the plan for redemption was set in place after satan was thrown off the board and lost his job. It was after he and his buddies were unceremoniously dumped out of Heaven that Plan B was implemented. Our all-knowing God knew that if He gave his man a free will, that he would fall and deserve death. So He had made ready an alternative plan. (God always has a plan.)

Plan B

We find *the plan* recorded in John 3:16:

For God so loved the world that He gave His only begotten Son, that whosoever believeth in Him should not perish, but have everlasting life (KJV).

That was Plan B.

The problem was that man deserved death, but God in His love sent Jesus to take upon Himself sin, sickness, poverty, and death. A perfect Man who did not deserve any of these things took the penalty of fallen man, paid the price, fought the battle, won the victory, and handed us the spoils of the war.

Satan, not knowing the details of the plan, fell into his part blindly. To put it concisely: Jesus volunteered to suffer, die, and go to hell for us. The Word says He did it "for the joy that was set before Him" (Hebrews 12:2). The joy was the reality of bringing you and me back into unbroken fellowship with God. Jesus became the last Adam and was "the firstborn among many brethren" (Romans 8:29). God got His family back.

When we accept His sacrifice, we are right back walking and talking one-on-one with our Father, taking back the dominion that Adam gave away. By the words of our mouth, we are now to inform satan that his lease is about up on the earth, and the children of God are moving back into position. Period. That's it in a nutshell.

More Good News

Not only that, but before Jesus went back to Heaven, He promised to send the Holy Spirit who would lead and guide *us* into all Truth. He would tell *us* what Father said. He would announce, declare, and disclose to us what would happen in the future. He said the very Spirit of Creator God would be with *us* constantly and would live in *us*. This Comforter would counsel, help, pray for, fight *our* battles, strengthen, and stand by *us*. He said that everything Father has was His and the Spirit would take what is His and give it to *us*. (Honestly, I am not making this up. Read John chapters 14 and 16 in the Amplified Bible.) As a friend of mine is fond of saying, "Sounds like a bird nest on the ground...we don't even have to fly to get there." How easy is that?

So what's the hold up? Journey on...

From Religion to Reality

When Jesus came to redeem the world, He introduced a new concept into the Jewish religion of His day. It was *the Father* concept. Somewhere in the previous 4,000 years man had totally lost the fact that God Almighty, El Shaddai, Jehovah, was also his *Creator Father.*

Along with losing the reality that God loved them like a Father, they also lost the intimacy, provision, and fellowship that went with that relationship. So when Jesus talked about "Father," He sent the religious world a message that we are still trying to swallow. It is much easier to think of God as an all-powerful, He-does-whatever-He-wants-to-do Deity, than to live in daily one-on-one relationship with a loving, benevolent, but just *Father* to whom we are accountable.

Jesus came as a Savior and a role model. Because He came through the womb of a woman, He was a flesh and blood man. In essence He spent His life upon the earth saying, "Okay, this is how it's done...I only do what I see *Father* doing. *Father* is always with Me. It's *Father* who does the works. *Father* lives continually in Me. I am in *Father* and you are in Me. *Father* and I are One.

It was this last statement that made "religion" so mad they wanted to kill Him. "What!" they screamed. "You make Yourself equal with God? Who do You think You are?" After a while Jesus just walked away from them. He had business to attend to. He did not have an identity crisis. He knew who He was and He certainly didn't need validation from them. After all, it wasn't His idea to make man equal with God. God did that all by Himself.

We must get it through our heads that there is only one *reality,* and that is our *Father's reality.* We belong to Him. We are created just like Him, and we are to act like Him. He created His man a tri-part being. We are a spirit; we have a soul; we live in a body. With our spirit we contact the spirit realm; with our soul we contact the mental realm; and with our bodies we contact the physical realm.

Our spirits are the real "us," the part that gets born again, the part that is the receptacle for the Holy Spirit of God. This is where He lives, and this is the *center* out of which we are to operate. Our souls are comprised of our mind, will, and emotions. Our bodies are simply the wonderfully designed vehicle for our spirits and souls. Its one job is to carry out the directions from the Spirit of God residing in our human spirit. The problem it has is, all the directions must come through our soul, and most of our souls have their own ideas of what it wants our bodies to do.

When we accept Jesus into our lives, the Holy Spirit moves into our spirits and we become new creatures. *In essence we are a brand new species of being.* For the most part, our soul and body does not change. We look the same, and (Lord help us) as a rule, we think the same.

Therein lies the problem for too many of God's beloved children. Here we are, new creations; we have the very breath of God (the Holy Spirit) in our spirit, but our soul—the way we think, the way we act, the way we feel—has not experienced a major change.

We may experience a brief born-again high when we are so wonderfully aware of what has happened that we even "feel" and "act" like who we say we are. At this point our *spirit*, the real us, has gained ascendancy and our *soul* shuts up trying to see how this new event is going to affect it. Then the honeymoon is over. The newness wears off, and the reality that we are going to have to "work out our own salvation" sets in. That's when the fear and trembling starts.

Instead of systematically setting about the process of renewing the mind (or soul) with the Word and practicing the presence of our Father, which is the only way to really get to know Him, we proceed to take this "new creation," this "free being," this "holy DNA" within us and conduct business as usual by living our life by the way we feel and think and by the force of our wills—in other words, out of our souls.

So we get up from our place of "reality" and begin to *think, What would Jesus do?* Depending on our past religious training, our culture, and our "programming" as a child, we come up with a whole scenario of don'ts. Jesus wouldn't get drunk, smoke, cuss, fornicate, cheat on His taxes, slap His wife, lie, scream at the children, eat too much cheesecake, break the speed limit, etc. etc. All true, no doubt.

We set about to *stop* all such subversive activity using the power of our soul—our wills—the very critter that got us into trouble in the first place. We make declarations, New Year's resolutions, go to church, go to Bible school, take courses, get counseled and prayed for, go through deliverance, cry, try to change, fail, wallow in guilt, feel defeated...then start the cycle over again.

Somehow, for so many of us, a pivotal truth has escaped us: When the Holy Spirit came into our human spirit, He didn't just come so we could go to Heaven someday. He is in there to be a helper, to stand beside us helping us to renew our minds, our wills, and our emotions. He is there to enable us to do what we have failed so miserably at. He is there to help us do what Jesus would do, help us think the way Jesus would think, and relate to Father the way Jesus related to Father.

Remember Jesus said, "I only do what I see Father doing...I only say what I hear Father saying." Jesus' soul was in perfect alignment with His spirit. His spirit, soul, and body worked in unity. That's how He could do the things He did.

The same thing holds true for the rest of the family, you and me. At the moment we begin living out of our spirits instead of our souls (what we think and feel), at the moment we get *centered*, able to differentiate between our spirits (where God lives) and our souls (where satan has access), at that precise moment we step into the *Peaceful Kingdom* where signs and wonders are common, everyday occurrences. This is our homeland. This is where we begin our journey in time.

Calvary has a universal and timeless message. It says, "Yes, everything is a mess, but you can start over now...clean slate...new beginning...the price is paid...take your inheritance...be who you were created to be."

Now you know why this book has found its way into your hands—to bring you home to the *golden dream in the heart of God*. Through His perfect Son He wanted to bring many sons and daughters back to the glory. This is our *destiny*. This is the way we are to live our lives out upon the earth—out of the bondage of "religion" into the freedom of our personal *"reality."* This is a *place called peace*. It is the *Kingdom of His Presence*. And from this *place*, the *glorious Church* will arise.

Prologue to Part Two

OUR JOURNEY INWARD

The Deepest Pain Is the Denial of Reality

The journey to *peace* has some serious wake-up calls along the way. The road can get pretty bumpy, especially as we traverse into the no-mans land of our souls. This is especially true of us Christian women. We have a tendency to appear to have it all together, but for the most part are oblivious or in denial about the power of our soul and its ability to control our lives.

As we begin our journey, we must first get our bearings. We must locate ourselves (point A). It is mandatory that we accept the fact that our lives have more questions, more missing pieces, and more failure than we know what to do with. We are embarking on a journey to explore the limitations that have successfully kept us out of the perfect, full-of-provision plan that Father has for our lives.

Before He can answer our questions—"What is wrong with me?" "What am I here for?" "What is my assignment?"—we need to answer a few questions ourselves.

Do I really want to change my life?

*Do I want **God's will**, or do I want what **I** want and God to bless what I want?*

Am I willing to do whatever it takes, regardless of how useless it seems to my mind, will, and emotions?

*Am I willing to admit (if only to God and myself) that I am not **all** that I portray to the world?*

How badly do I want to be free from the cycle of fear that keeps me from going forward?

*Do I have all the love, joy, peace, money, self-confidence, security, healing, wholeness, and direction I need, or do I know deep in my heart that there is **more** for me?*

We will never go somewhere else until we get fed up with where we are. We can attain only what we are willing to pursue. I believe it is time for the women of God to be free to walk in all the light, provision, and anointing we must have to fulfill *the assignment* we were sent to earth to accomplish. Father is counting on us.

The women in this last-day Church will make a major impact before Jesus returns. You and I are a part of that gifted, powerful force. Are you ready to move a few mountains? If so, prayerfully sign this agreement, and we will begin *The Search for Peace*.

Read carefully before you sign. This is the beginning of your *quality decisions*.

My Commitment to Myself

I _____ **understand I am undertaking** the first part of an intense guided journey toward my own reality, my call, my mission, my personal assignment.

I _____ **further understand that this commitment** includes daily and weekly readings, meditations, and exercises that I will complete…even if my soul (mind, will, and emotions) have a fit.

I _____ **understand that this course** may raise issues, emotions, and truths that have been deeply buried for a very long time. But I am determined to know the truth and the truth I know will set me free.

I _____ **commit for the duration** of this course to the nonnegotiable disciplines of spending time daily *practicing the presence of God* and writing the prescribed Word assignments in my journal.

I _____ **realize this is a commitment to myself,** and I am so serious enough about wanting *MORE*, that I fully intend to keep it.

_____   _____

Your Signature   Date

Old Things Have Passed Away, Behold All Things Are New

Well, I guess we are ready, except for one thing...let's do ourselves a favor and lighten our load. For the duration of this study, let us make a *quality decision* to be open to *new ways* of communicating with God (i.e., how we talk to Him and how He may be speaking to us). Remember that we are moving into *new territory* and it is a *new day*. Nothing and no one can hold us back...except us, and we have just signed a commitment not to do that anymore.

About Our Journey Inward

On this particular *journey to our Peaceful Kingdom,* we will be passing through a dozen other *kingdoms.* Each one must be passed all the way through. Why? To get to the other side.

On our *journey* we will discover, explore, and conquer one *kingdom* a week. Some of these individual territories will personally impact us more than others, but all will reveal a different way the enemy has used to keep the *assignments* from the Body of Christ, particularly women. Once we are on the other side of each of these *roadblock kingdoms,* we will be able to affirm, "Been there...done that...and my life proves it."

About Weekly Assignments

As I have traveled toward my own inner peace and have had the honor to guide many other women, Father has taught us a few things that have helped move us forward and keep our focus. Weekly Assignments are one of them.

I received a Word from Him concerning these assignments. This is what He said:

> *The details unveiled in the assignments are pivotal to My leading and healing This is why your soul belongs to your human spirit inseparable for eternity. My wisdom, love, grace, abundance, and mercy flow out of your human spirit via your soul. Just as your body has a physical brain that processes everything, your spirit has a soul that processes everything. Even if your brain is damaged in one area, other areas can continue to work fine. Likewise, a damaged soul can also have areas that work fine. The assignments reveal areas of damage in your soul.*

46

Brain damage can be irreversible in the natural. Soul damage can be irreversible in the natural. But nothing is irreversible in My presence.

May I suggest you travel (or read) through each kingdom on a specific day of the week (for instance, Sunday), and complete the assignments during the rest of the week.

Take Special Care Not to Neglect the Three Foundational Exercises

1. *Practice the Presence of God for at **least** the suggested time each day.*

   This is done by *centering* into our human spirit where He abides. Our spirit, the "real us," is generally centered in the mid-section of our bodies. The Word says that *"out of our bellies shall flow rivers of living water"* (John 7:38 KJV). It also refers to our spirit as the *"inner man"* (Eph 3:16). So by simply getting quiet and becoming aware that He is *there* is *practicing His presence.* With enough practice, this can be done in the busiest of busy places, or in the midst of horrendous attacks from satan. He is available 24/7 to talk to you and to listen.

2. *Write the Word of God in a journal and make it up close and personal.*

   This can be most fun and so simple to do. It is literally believing that what the Word says is the real Truth... and it is talking to you personally.

3. *Follow the assignments at the end of each week's journey.*

   These will vary week to week. All are powerful, and if done with a sincere desire for enlightenment, will help unlock your potential for the *call of God* upon your life.

   The only way we can "reprogram" our souls (renew our minds) is replace *beliefs* with *Truth.* That is the goal of the assignments.

The Crystal Cup

I hold out to you my soul
An empty crystal cup,
Praying you will
Fill it with kindness
With good...with love.

I watch your eyes
Searching your heart,
Weary of what you might
Place in the recesses
Of...my emptiness.

I wait... hand trembling
For your decision.
What will it be this time?
Life or death?
Light or darkness?

Part Two:
The Kingdom of the Soul

SEARCHING SOUL SYNDROME

This kingdom is actually our place of departure. This is where most of us have lived out our lives. It's not that we were born here. To the contrary, our hometown is a place called *Peace* and there is precious little of that in this neck of the woods. Be that as it may, here we are, due to the fact we were created to search for our *place* in life and didn't know where else to look. The ruler of this *kingdom* is known far and wide for making boxes. Yes, boxes. He makes them, and we crawl in them and live miserably ever after.

Searching for *our place* begins early. We want to be validated. We turn to those around us to give us a sense of worth. We want someone's eyes to light up when we enter a room. More often than not, the people we are looking hopefully at to fill this core need are too busy searching for their own sense of place...hence, they never see the hunger in our eyes.

No one escapes the *searching soul syndrome*. Because we look for fulfillment from other searching souls, people consistently bail out on us. When we trustingly hold the crystal cup of our soul out to someone who has nothing to give, the results can be devastating. Sometimes they slap it out of our hands treating it like a cheap tin cup worth nothing. It gets stepped on, battered, bent. Other times they try to scrape even the tiny drops of love, hope, and dreams out of our cup to fill their own empty spaces. Emptiness cannot fill emptiness, but emptiness will always be filled with something—if not affirmation and love, then rejection and hurt.

Our soul is incredibly and exactly like a computer—it only knows whatever is programmed into it. Whatever is deposited into it will eventually be downloaded into our lives. Pain in...pain out; love in...love out; acceptance in...acceptance out; rejection in...rejection out. This programming constitutes our "core beliefs."

We always act based on our core beliefs. They are the foundational bricks we lay out to build our lives upon. They can be negative or positive; most of us have a combination. When we have experienced rejection, abuse, or trauma, the core beliefs deposited in our souls (or mind, will, and emotions) can be wrong, warped, and fundamentally self-destructive. They keep us in a box and the box has a lid on it. This leads to denial, and we live in the land of illusions.

If we have had a lot of emotional pain, after a while, we consciously or unconsciously, decide it doesn't really matter. We tuck our battered soul away building emotional walls around it as a protective mechanism. The building material for our walls are made from rejection. We keep adding to this edifice all our lives. Every time we are wounded we add another brick.

We can get so proficient at building walls that we do it subconsciously. Even if we are not abused, we may perceive we are and it is the same difference. More bricks. Even self-inflicted pain will become building material. The end result is the same. We put in place the core beliefs that will keep us limited, our potential stymied, our dreams colorless, and our lives lived out in a neat box where everything is controlled, predictable, and consequently, oh so safe.

Positive core beliefs are built in when we have been loved and validated. In these areas of our souls we shine...unless of course the negative outweighs the positive. Then just when we begin to feel good about ourselves, the negative beliefs say to the positive beliefs, "Just who do you think you are kidding?" The negative programming in us will interrupt and answer, "Nobody," then we slink away with one more disappointment, one more failure, one more time we have sabotaged ourselves.

Samples Please...

Here is an exhausting, if not exhaustive, list of negative core beliefs taken from my life and the lives of others, and the mortar we use to hold them in place. All are gleaned from life experiences or wounds created by words deposited into our souls.

All men are _____ (fill in the blank) users... abusive...self-centered...non-promise keepers....

I don't need anybody.

My marriage failed...it must be my fault.

My dad never loved me and/or abused me. Why would a Father God care about me? What is a father anyway?

I am too fat...too thin...too short...too tall to be beautiful...so why try?

My husband flirts with other women...it must be my fault.

If I had more time...money...energy, I would paint a picture... start a business...learn to play the piano...create order in my home...play with the kids...write a letter...read the Bible...go to med school...write in my journal, but I don't have time, money or energy.

If I had been able to love him enough...give enough...pray enough...be patient long enough...be submissive enough..., he would not have drunk...taken drugs...beat me...called me ugly names...left me for the other woman...or made my life hell on earth. (Again, fill in your own blanks.)

If I had more education, money, freedom, I would be happy. But I don't, I can't, and I'm not.

They said I was stupid...a failure...a bad girl...ugly...bipolar...and I've proved them right.

And the sad self-destructive symphonies play on, all designed to keep us in a box and away from our *assignment*. Granted, there is a certain security in not getting out of the box. We may very well be miserable, but at least we know *what* we are...miserable.

Being the *pilgrims* that we are, we do get out of the box sometimes and begin the journey. But the moment we take a step toward our *Search for Peace,* such as going back to school, getting a job, creating art, joining a Bible study group, beginning an exercise program, or doing this course, a whole artesian well of negative core beliefs erupt to stop our progress.

Such as...

I don't have time for this.

My mother...father...husband...whoever...would not approve.

He might leave me if I change. (Yes, he might...but he could go with you. That's his choice.)

If I lock myself in the bathroom for 30 minutes a day to practice the presence of God, they (whoever "they" are) will think I'm crazy.

Maybe I am crazy.

If I find out what motivates me, I might be worse off.

Nobody is going to believe I talk to God and He answers me.

I don't even believe it.

I sin. I have addictions—alcohol...food...codependency... nicotine.... God will never tell me my assignment until I quit _____ . (Fill in the blank.)

And last, but not least...

It is too late for me.

Of course, the stock question to that one is, "If you don't get out of the box, where will you be this time next year?" Answer: "Right where you are now, in the same box peeking out."

Bottom line—IT IS NEVER TOO LATE.

Grandma Taught It and We Bought It

Other negative core beliefs are imparted into us by well-meaning adults who pass on information handed down to them. In an effort to ensure her a "proper" future, a grandmother pulls her lovely, newly blossoming, adolescent granddaughter aside and says, "You don't want to gain too much weight or you will not find a husband to love you."

Confused because she didn't do anything to get these new curves, the little girl in an almost-woman's body, begins a lifelong battle with her weight. Her self-image becomes so deeply scarred that at 50 years old and 20 pounds overweight she has a daily struggle accepting the love her devoted husband has for her. She cannot see that he loves her for who she really is—a remarkable, beautiful, fun-to-be-with woman. And it all began almost 40 years ago when a beloved grandma whispered "words of advice" into the ear of a twelve-year-old. Result: fear motivated, negative core beliefs.

Then there are the parents who become our role models whether we like it or not. An abusive mother teaches her daughter "how to mother." An abusive father teaches his daughter "what to expect" in a husband. She may hate what he is, but unconsciously he's all she knows to look for.

A girl who experiences shame and humiliation by her earthly father will struggle with trusting a heavenly Father. The core belief that "fathers are abusive and use their kids for their own gratification" is a widespread and emotionally, not to mention spiritually, damaging concept among the daughters of God today. She can spend her life looking for a "real father" and continually draw to herself "users"…until she meets *Father*. The way we relate to our earthly fathers, most of the time, is how we approach our heavenly Father. There are few exceptions. Core beliefs may not be true. But because of their source (i.e., people who matter), they become the axis on which our personal world revolves. Unconfronted, they will undermine and effectively stop any progress toward our *assignment*. Our goal here is to confront them.

Negative beliefs are not *truth*; they are *beliefs*. Just because we believe something does not necessarily make it true. They are bricks. Bricks and bricks and more bricks…held together by mortar also filled with rejection. These are the substance of the walls that have kept our lives in a box and our future predictably the same as our past—when all the time *the golden dream in the heart of God* is waiting on the horizon to blaze forth in brilliant power and beauty.

Oh Those Boxes! Also Known as Comfort Zones

Armed with enough bricks and mortar, gleefully supplied by satan and courtesy of the people closest to us, we can build a very substantial box. From that box we live and move and have our being. This box always has a lid. Sometimes we lift the lid and peek out. Outside the box, *our reality, the reason we are here, our assignment, the call* beckons us with its radiance. But...if...only...maybe ...someday.

Once we have our box built, we get inside and set up housekeeping with our wounded soul in charge. From our exalted position of utter blindness, we defiantly dare anybody to tell us we are wrong or that things can change. What we have built is a stronghold against the truth. Sometimes we open our box and peek out, hoping against hope that this time maybe it will be different. As prisoners of hope, we ask for prayer, go to church, read the right books, and study the Word of God...that is the real *us* reaching out for help. But because we don't understand how our souls create our lives, we make little headway.

We do venture a peek out of our box and look at *Truth* by lifting the lid on Sunday morning, or when "Brother Anointed" comes to town, or when we read an inspirational book. While we are under the influence of an anointed minister, we *know* we are overcomers. But the moment those golden nuggets of Truth slam into our negative core beliefs, our battered soul says, "That won't work for me"...**SLAM**... back in the box it goes taking our spirits and bodies with it. Inside the box our soul carefully fits the lid down, tapes it shut, and proceeds to create another brick of disappointment. Out of the box, *faith* would have to kick in, putting the ball back in our court, but a box is much more comfortable and a lot less work.

Because of the condition of our souls, we even sometimes take a life-giving *word* and filter it through a whole collection of wrong beliefs. The result is pollution. Too many of us live out our Christian lives, operate in the ministry, preach, lead churches, and prophesy out of our souls instead of our spirits; and we never know the difference. If by some miracle of God's grace and mercy (and it does happen), He is able to bypass a negative part of our souls in a moment of Divine Inspiration, after the moment passes we still end up bringing reproach upon the Body of Christ by the way we continue to conduct our lives out of our negative core beliefs.

There are times we would swear we have, "Thus saith the Lord," when in reality it is, "Thus saith my soul." I know, I've done it. That's the reason we get a *word* today and six months or six years later we discover that our *word* was not from God, but possibly a word from satan spoken through our souls, or more likely it was our soul giving its opinion—the same soul that lives in, and runs our life out of a prison box of emotional pain.

As the apostle Paul says, *"O wretched man that I am! Who shall deliver me?"* (Romans 8:24 KJV). Thank God there is help...God has a plan. (Remember, God always has a plan.)

Our Divine Helper

What we can't get away from is our born-again spirit where God lives. It is the still small voice of the Holy Spirit in our spirits that motivates us to lift the lid off our boxes. Our spirits were made in His image. Our spirit is *who* we really are. We were created to daily soar into new heights in unity and in partnership with our Creator Father. Our spirit will never, never, never be content, fulfilled, or at peace as long as it is held captive by a renegade soul full of preconceived ideas.

Consequently, we, us, the real person will never be content or at peace until we have the insight to know that we are *royalty*, a ruler in the *Kingdom of Peace*; and Father does not want us to live in this dark cramped space. He has more for us. At that point we will take our authority, flip the lid off that box, and inform our body and our soul, "Listen up...I'm in charge here and we are getting out of this self-destructive, dream-stealing, pain-filled prison of emotional garbage."

Decision Dance

I danced between the two.
In Faith, Spirit danced with me
Playing celestial music
Choreographing my every step
Catching me when I leaped.

In Fear, I danced alone.
A black shadow
Standing in the wings
The music threatening
When I leaped...shadow laughed.

Assignments

THE KINGDOM OF THE SOUL

1. **Read Hebrews 4:12.** It clearly states exactly what we need to tell the difference between the soul, the spirit, and the body.

    *For the **word of God** is quick, and powerful, and sharper than any twoedged sword, piercing even to the **dividing** asunder of **soul and spirit**, and of the joints and marrow [body], and is a discerner of the thoughts and intents of the heart* (KJV, emphasis added).

    In layman's terms this means: As we study the Word of God, it is powerful (able) to divide, separate, make a distinction between our soul (where we store all the "stuff"), and our spirits where the Holy Spirit, our Divine Guide lives.

2. **Go back and read the samples of negative core beliefs.** Do any of them ring a bell? When you want to step out of the box what do you *hear* from the past that stops you?

    When and from whom did you first hear this voice?

    Note these in your journal…they will come in handy later.

3. **Be honest—what is the first word that comes to your mind when I say "Father"?**

    What is/was your relationship with your earthly father? Write it down.

Is it possible that when you first got saved, your past colored how you felt about your heavenly Father?

For years I talked only to Jesus. That "loving heavenly Father" deal was beyond me. But then I got to know Him. That's when I found true Love.

4. **The Word *Up Close and Personal:***

In your journal write John 3:16; make it personal to you.

You may be surprised and at times shocked when you do this exercise. What you are doing is taking the "religion" out of the Word and inserting reality.

Suggested Phrasing: "Father loves *me* so much that He gave His Son Jesus so that I may have a wonderful life now and forever."

Find another *special word* in the Bible especially from Father and write it *Up Close and Personal.*

Psalm 23 is a good one. It begins, "The Lord is *my* Shepherd, I don't want for anything" (*Up Close and Personal*).

Read them over and over this week. Speak them aloud, especially when you have a flare-up of a negative core belief. The revelation behind this exercise is the beginning of reprogramming ourselves to think about *us* the way Father thinks about *us.*

Example:

If *they* said, "You don't know anything about anything," and Jesus said, "*The Holy Spirit will guide you into all the Truth*" (John 16:13), that does not sound as if you are uninformed to me. We are the deciding factor. **Are we to believe *them* or Jesus?**

5. **Practice the Presence:** *Each day* this week set aside five minutes to get totally alone and talk to Father. Say anything you want. He is not going to fall off the Throne even if you're mad, sad, glad, bad, fed up, or think this whole exercise is stupid. He is your Father, and He is like no other father you have ever met.

After you have spoken what is in your heart (do it in every-day words just as you would talk to a friend), listen to the still small voice inside your spirit. The Spirit Voice will come out of your midsection, not your head. He is there (in your human spirit) to tell you everything you need to know. **Expect Him to communicate to you...He will.**

Record in your journal, what you said and His reply. Give Him equal time.

6. **Use your journal for a daily meditation.** Share your new insights with your study group or a friend. Or just talk to Father about them.

The Kingdom of Decisions

DAILY DECISIONS ARE HOLY MOMENTS

Having just come from a guided tour of our souls, we are now ready to take on the territory that will give us the forward thrust we need to launch into our future. In truth, what we gain in this *kingdom* will go with us on the whole trip and far beyond until Jesus returns.

A powerful Word about what we are to do with our souls comes from the apostle Paul in Romans 12:2. Lets look at it *Up Close and Personal* as he writes:

> *Don't be conformed to the way everybody else thinks (for that matter, especially what they think about you). But be transformed (changed) by the entire renewal of your mind (soul). Take on new ideas and new attitudes.* **When** *you do that, you will be able to prove for yourself what is* **the good,** *and* **the acceptable,** *and* **the perfect** *will of God for your life. Even the* **thing** *He has planned especially for you* (paraphrased from the Amplified Bible, *Up Close and Personal*).

Quality Decision... or Not

The first thing decision (NOTE: I know the word is over used but the point is we have to make a decision to make a decision) confronting us on our *journey* is to make a decision. Not just a "Yeah-yeah, I'll do it if I have time" decision, but a *quality decision* from which we will not turn back. If we expect *change* in our lives, we must use our God-given free will to decide to *do* something about it. There will never, and I stress *NEVER*, be any noticeable change in our lives if we don't make a *quality decision* to renew our minds (or reprogram our souls) with the Word of God.

I'm not talking about just "new information." We receive new information every time we go to church, read a book, or listen to a tape. New information doesn't renew our mind. Change is the evidence of a renewed mind. When the *information* brings about *change,* then our mind is renewed.

Renewing our minds is a process. It is not an event...a book...a dream...a vision. Nor is it a "Thus saith the Lord" to you personally, even if "the word" is delivered by a prophet of God who is known far and wide for being able to read your mail. Prophetic *words* to us will not effect change unless we use them as a catalyst to get into *the Word* and renew our minds in the areas they address.

Change doesn't happen just because we desire it or even need it. Our lives are transformed *only* by the renewing of our minds or souls. Paul was saying that it is with our "new attitude" that we prove for ourselves what is God's perfect will for our lives. To know that we are indeed "renewing our minds" and not just "gathering information," it must be apparent that *change* has transpired. When *"old things are passed away and all things are new,"* then our mind is renewed—not before.

Change...Who Me?

Right about now a little (soulish) voice may be saying, "Sure okay, that's all well and good for some people, but *I* know the Word... and *I* don't have soulish issues. I am motivated only by the Spirit of God. *I* pray, read the Word, teach, preach, have the gifts flowing in *my* ministry, so all this is a big waste of time for *me."* Fair enough...but before you throw this book on the pile of other self-help books on your spiritual bookshelf, take a few minutes to ask yourself these questions. (By the way, the big *I* monolog I just shared was once *my* opinion of *me,* and I was a bona fide, card-carrying, soulish mess.)

If you can respond to all of these questions with the answer "no," then go ahead and pitch the book; it won't do you a bit of good. Better yet, pass it on to the people that you *know* have problems.

Symptoms of a Soul-Run Life

1. *Do I ever find myself being defensive or have a tendency to blame others for my problems?*

2. Do I have issues or problems with some people...all people?

3. Do I allow people to walk on me, or say unkind things to, or about me...abuse me?

4. Do I have a need to control and have things my way? Do I have to be right and try to convince others to agree with me?

5. When I am caught doing wrong, am I sorry for what I did...or am I sorry I got caught?

6. Do I have a hard time staying in church unless I am in charge of something?

7. Do I constantly need prayer and get in every prayer line hoping this time it will work?

8. Do I have trouble knowing it is God speaking? Do I wonder is it Him or me?

9. Are there areas in my past that still cause anger...pain...sadness...fear?

10. Do I sometimes feel "called by God" to straighten others out, or try to "fix them"?

11. Do I have problems with my finances, family, husband, children, or neighbors?

12. Do I hide things from the people around me—food...purchases...secrets?

13. Do I go out of my way trying to impress people with my spirituality, money, or success?

14. When an abuser from my past surfaces, does my stomach get that familiar knot in it?

15. Do I have a temper, or compulsive habits like mindless shopping...lying ... escaping real life with too much television, the internet, or sleep?

16. Do I lack "focus"? Am I going one way today and another way tomorrow?

17. Do I have any addictive behaviors...drinking...smoking...overeating...drug abuse...illicit sex?

18. *Have I had a problem maintaining my healing, after I know I am healed?*

19. *Do I consistently, year after year, run into the same kind of problems —employment changes...failed marriages...money... strife... loneliness...rejection...illnesses...church hopping?* (This is a tricky one because we convince ourselves that "God" is leading us on.)

20. *Am I afraid of failure...success...sickness...death...people... commitment...job changes?*

If you had to honestly answer "yes" to any of these questions, then you better hold steady a while before you pass this book on to the "needy souls" you live with. Because Dear Soul Sister, every one of these symptoms are rooted and grounded in your mind, will, and emotions, otherwise known as your soul. They are symptoms of a fragmented soul fighting for dominion. It wants to run your life, and if you answered "yes" to more than five of these questions, it is doing a credible job.

The amazingly good news is that these symptoms are not in your spirit (the "real you"). What is in your spirit is the Spirit of Almighty God, Creator of the universe. And He is there to help us get our renegade soul healed and into position. All it takes is a *decision* on our part. We are always only *one* decision away from whatever we want in life...only one.

Do we want our Holy Guide to lead us into the most beautifully dazzling life, full of every kind of provision beyond what we can ask or think? Do we want to be able to act like who we say we are? Do we want to become "more than a conqueror"? Do we want to get into position for the *endtime glory* as God does His grandest thing upon the earth? Or do we continue to play "twenty questions" with the devil?

I know your answer.

You're going for it.

Take the Land

We, the women of God, are well able to "take the land," and as the daughter of Caleb told her father in Joshua 15:19, *"Give me a present. Since you have set me in the [dry] Negeb, give me also springs of water.*

And he gave her the [sloping field with] upper and lower springs." That girl got tired of living in the desert and like a real smart daughter, she went to Daddy and asked for springs of water...and got them. She made a *quality decision,* and it paid off. I believe when you signed that *agreement with yourself,* a few pages back, you too made a *quality decision* and the payoff is just down the road. A *decision* is an open door into *reality.* We have just gone to "Papa" and asked for "springs of living water" to wash through our souls...and He can't refuse His daughters when they are serious. Once we make a *decision,* Heaven will back us up. We have made *a decision* to *change,* and we will never be the same. The *process* has begun.

Remember: Daily decisions are holy moments. When we make them, Heaven stands to attention.

The Habitation of Dragons

Paralyzed I saw him coming,
A dragon of fear
Breathing black fire from hell.
I took his flame
And started a fire of my own,
Trying to thaw my frozen soul
And only succeeded
In getting colder still.

Assignments

THE KINGDOM OF DECISIONS

1. **Read over "My Commitment to Myself" in the Prologue to Part Two.** How does it make you feel? Scared…committed…determined…empowered?

2. **Honestly record your answers to the 20 questions in this section.** (Some of them may be an honest "no," but if there are some answers that are "yes" and a few "maybes," you have just red-flagged a section of your soul that satan has been attacking.

    (When I checked off the ones I personally have had to deal with—presently and in the past— I had to answer "yes" to 19 out of the 20. That's how I got my "professional soulish mess" status.)

3. **Copy the following "Keys to Change Affirmations" in your journal.**

    I make a quality decision to change.

    I turn over my will (soul) completely to God.

    I'm tired of the way things are…I want to change.

    I will learn more of the Word by making it *Up Close and Personal*.

    I will diligently apply Truth to my life day after day and pay attention to the decisions I make daily during those holy moments)

I will defend my mind (soul) against negative thoughts.

I will be selective to what I expose myself to...people and world influences.

I will be teachable...no excuses.

I will depend on Father for support and the Holy Spirit to guide me.

I will set boundaries around my decisions.

READ THEM ALOUD SO YOU CAN HEAR THEM.

SPOKEN WORDS CREATE REALITY.

4. **Spend ten minutes *each day* this week *practicing the presence of God*.**

The Kingdom of Fear

FEAR...SATAN'S WEAPON OF CHOICE

The *Kingdom of Fear* has a long and dark history. It began in the polluted heart of satan and is populated by a vast multitude of God's children. We have been convinced by evil that *fear* is a natural state of habitation. It is not.

There is nothing "natural" about living in fear that something terrible is going to happen to your children. There is nothing "natural" about being afraid to pick up the TV remote control because that might be the trigger that sets off your abusive husband. There is nothing "natural" about covering up the terrible things we live with, in fear of what people will think. There is nothing "natural" about having to spend our days tiptoeing around the volcanic nature of the people in our lives. There is nothing "natural" about the gnawing sickness in the pit of our stomach when we hear a certain voice. This is not "natural" for the children of *Father*. This is hell on earth, and it is *not* natural.

This *dark kingdom* is infested with "dragons." They will singe your soul and leave your dreams in ashes. The evil fire they breathe at us is fueled by *fear*. The heat from their fiery blast is the furnace in which we make the bricks to build our walls. *Fear* inspired. *Fear* formed. *Fear* created.

The dragons have one master, and his one motivation is to delay, if not stop, us on our *Search for Peace*. He wants to mess up the God-appointed assignment we were created to carry out

Ever since he messed up his own assignment, he has been hell-bent on messing up every body else's. His weapon of choice is fear. Remember the first words out of Adam's mouth after his major goof-up in the Garden of Eden? When God asked him, "Adam where are you?" he replied, "I was *afraid* and I hid myself." God is still speaking to His children, "Where are you? Why are you not walking in My plan?" Our answer is the same as Adam's, "I am afraid and I am hiding." The first Adam got us where we are; the "second Adam," Jesus Christ, got us where we ought to be. Jesus came to eradicate the fear and its effects from our spirits, souls, and bodies. His first sermon in His hometown clearly stated *His mission, His assignment.*

You will find the details in Isaiah 61. Here is the paraphrase *Up Close and Personal,* especially for women.

I Have Come

I have come to bring good news to the poor. You don't have to be afraid of poverty anymore. I have come to bind up and heal the brokenhearted. You don't have to live in the past pain and rejection that caused your broken heart. I am here to cover your wounds and heal you. I have come to set captives free and open the prison of the soul-dominated box you live in, to unbind your spirit so you can soar, to give you joy instead of grief...beauty in place of the ashes of your past. Dry your tears, Little One, quit grieving...I have come to console you, to give you peace. I have come to give you a beautiful new irides-cent white garment of praise to replace the shroud made of heavy burdensome failure. To Me, you are strong, magnificent, distinguished... a royal princess. I am proud of you. I planted you and I tend you like a rose in My garden of delight. You bring Me honor. Together you and your sisters will rebuild the ancient ruins of your lives and renew the old waste places. All the devastations of your past are over....

He said, "I have come. And P.S. You don't have to be afraid anymore."

Fear, satan's weapon of choice is in reality the *only* major problem we will ever have. (We will go through the *kingdom of deception* later which is also devastating, but even that is motivated by fear.)

Did God Really Say?

Fear contaminates faith, and nothing works in the *Kingdom of God* without faith. We can't please *Father* without faith. As women of God, however, we do have faith. We had to have faith to get saved. We *know* Jesus died for us and we accept His sacrifice, all by faith. It's when the rubber hits the road and we have to put our faith on the line that we screech to a halt and allow the dragons breathing fear to take aim at us. At that point we are right back in the Garden with Eve hearing satan whisper, "Did God really say?" planting doubt which creates fear.

> *Did God really say, He would "supply all your needs"? So why is the electricity bill past due?*

> *Did God really say, "By His stripes you are healed"? So why do you have cancer?*

> *Did God really say, "Your children are taught of the Lord, and great is the peace of your children"? So why are they on drugs?*

"Did God really say…did God really say…did God really say?" Sometimes I think satan has a limited vocabulary, seeing as since the Garden of Eden he hasn't come up with a different phrase. I suppose he adheres to the concept of, "If it's not broke, don't fix it," and this mode of operation is definitely still working quite effectively in the Body of Christ. He comes to steal the Word by planting fear; we take the fear and begin to worry, which produces more fear.

Worry is the art of meditating on the lies of the devil. From years of first-class, state-of-the-art training from our parents, some of us have developed worry into a fine art. Really good Christians who would never lie, steal, or commit adultery, consistently fear or worry. (Call it what you will, they are part and parcel of the same thing.) Worry is sin. It's saying that God's Word is not true or I'm not worthy to receive, so He probably won't do it for me, which is basically the same thing.

When we worry, we are choosing to believe a lie from hell over the Word of Almighty God. After all, He has given us piles of promises that refute any lie satan whispers. The dragons blast us with a fear that might say, "Your children are going to get killed." If our minds are not renewed in that area to *know* exactly what the Bible says about our children and the power of God to keep our children safe, we will begin to meditate on the lies of the devil. The only way to meditate on lies is to worry.

Meditate simply means to roll over and over in your mind. When we meditate the Word, we roll it over and over in our minds. Worry is doing the same about a lie. Of course, most of us have had a negative core belief deposited in our souls that states, "If you don't worry, you don't care." How warped is that?—especially when the Bible says some 365 times in one way or another, "Fear not," which could be paraphrased *Up Close and Personal* as, "Don't worry, Girl, I've got you covered."

Do you get the feeling this book is just one big reality check? All I can say is that it was definitely for me. When I got serious enough to *do* something about my life, God got involved in my decision and began to point out areas in my soul that were motivated by fear, which was, in truth, a goodly portion. The bottom line of what He taught me was that if I didn't do something about the fear that satan instigates in my life, nothing would ever be done. I could choose to believe satan's dart of fear or God's Words of Life. I could *meditate* on whatever I wanted to, and it would come to pass in my life. I was the deciding factor. Period. End of discussion.

Caution: Fear at Work

Not only does fear affect our souls (our minds, wills, and emotions) killing our dreams and our future, it is also a major medical issue. *Stress* is the effects of fear upon our bodies. Fear generates stress, which generates high blood pressure, which generates heart disease and a whole slew of other stress related diseases. Even cancer and crippling arthritis have been linked to fear.

People pay multimillions of dollars each year to psychologists, psychiatrists, medical doctors, counselors, and therapists trying to combat the effects of fear. The professions that search for the causes behind the problems generally discover some form of fear. A fire-breathing dragon has been there.

There is another multimillion dollar industry geared solely to "Stress Management." This includes meditation, exercise, aromatherapy, massage therapy, reflexology (having your feet massaged), and the list goes on. All have a degree of truth and will work to a certain extent. Most of them I have tried and enjoyed immensely. But all they could do is temporarily "manage" the effects of stress on my body—not remove it.

Mentally, fear produces phobias. *Phobia* is defined in the dictionary as "an obsessive or irrational fear or anxiety of some subject or situation." Television psychologist Dr. Phil McGraw says that there is only one 'phobia' with many manifestations, including germ phobia, height phobia, claustrophobia. He believes the one 'phobia' that people have is 'the fear of not being in control.'

When fear is well developed by a wounded soul who is trying to protect itself from future pain, it creates what is commonly known these days as a "control freak." These victims of multiple onslaughts of the dragons are aggressive, domineering, controlling people who must have their own way. If things are not done "their way," all hell breaks loose either around them, manifesting the disorders in their mind, wills, and emotions; or if internalized, the fear will wreck havoc in their bodies.

Fear is the seedbed for every phobia, control issue, and paranoia known to man. Fear gives birth to more fear. Victims as well as their abusers all operate from fear. Fear drives victims into being abusers. They may become aggressive abusers, who use verbal and physical power, or passive-aggressive, meek appearing people who control others by guilt, tears, or psychosomatic illnesses. Then there are the victims who are codependents. These wounded souls enable and help their abuser continue to abuse them.

I have firsthand knowledge of how a control freak can emerge from a victim status. My own history is riddled with control issues. Born to a passive-aggressive mom and a volatile abusive father, as early as three years old I recall incidents of furniture smashing violence and my mother being beaten.

I learned early to withdraw into myself, stay out of the way, and try to keep other people happy. Time passed and as each new person entered my life, I experienced fear of not pleasing, fear of not doing enough, fear that the sexual, emotional, and physical abuse was my fault. Fear paralyzed me. I didn't know how to say no to anything. So I lost my life, myself, the essence of the real "me" in the whirlwind of being nice…submissive… trying to please…cooperating…keeping the peace…until I had no control over anything except "my stuff."

"My stuff," meant my immediate environment, the way I arranged things in my home. If I placed a candlestick here, a vase of flowers there, and laid a book at a certain angle to perfectly compose a still-life of order, heaven help the person who moved anything to any degree.

I had learned passive-aggressive real well at my mother's knee, and while I rarely lost my temper, I would get mad. Real mad. When someone moved "my stuff," a furious anger would rise up in me. I could walk into a room I had arranged and tell in half a second if anything was even one inch out of place.

Weird? Oh yes.

Unusual? Not really.

A soul issue? You bet.

I know now that the compulsive, desperate attempt to control my environment was directly related to the fact that I had no control over anything else in my life. Other people made all my decisions— how I was treated physically and emotionally, where I lived and how long, if I had money and how much. I feared losing the last bit of control I had in my life. Every other decision I tried to make was met with disapproval or outright criticism. My house, my stuff, my environment was the only place I felt safe in making a decision. Actually, Father created us to have "dominion," and this was the only "dominion" I could get my hands on.

Majoring in Minors

The anger in me was the telling key. Majoring in minors? Definitely. But minors was all I had left. This one control was the sole expression of *me*. I tried all my life to fit into a mold that would make "them" happy. It was as though I had given custody of my life over to someone else and only had visitation rights. When it appeared that even my visitation rights were being tampered with, my soul had a fit.

The problem with giving in to that kind of fear and becoming a victim is we place the ownership of our life, the real *us*, into the hands of someone else. We live to please, even if they are wrong, even if they are abusive, even if *who* we are dies.

An even bigger problem with being a victim of the dragons' blasts of fear is, not only do we lose who *we are*, but we lose who we *might have been*. Victims are not allowed to dream…unless of course the dream meets the approval of the controlling abuser.

You Can't…Not Now…Not Ever

"You can't run a business because you can't handle money." And the *God-given dream* of opening a tea room or shop dies. (Or if the dream, by some manifested miracle, meets their approval, you can do the work and they will handle the money.)

"You can't get a good job with that degree…you've just wasted time and money going to school." And the *call of God* to touch lives as a pre-school teachers dies.

"You can't be an artist…you will starve. Get into med-school." This statement is generally made from parents of a brilliant child who want only the best for her. The doctor graduate pulls down a six-figure income and is perfectly miserable. Ability? Yes. *God-given assignment*? No.

"You can't write, you can't spell, you can't get an agent. Who would want to read anything you have to say anyway?" You can't…you can't…you can't. And the books, stories, or poetry that the Holy Spirit has imparted into your heart will never manifest, will never be presented to the world, will never have a chance to change lives. One more dream is dead. Fear won.

If this happens long enough, we lose our ability to dream, and the world has lost the *golden dream in the heart of God* that was uniquely ours.

The dragons breathe on as we exit this dream-stealing kingdom…fear of failure…fear of not being loved…fear of man…fear of success…fear of getting out of the box. Fear…the *only* weapon satan has that can steal our promises from Father. But dragons also have something to fear, and that is the fear of Light. They may breathe fire; however, it is a black fire and they live in the darkness.

Our defense is simple, but labor-intensive… replace the fear with Faith. If this agenda against us is to succeed, it must have our acceptance. Fear is optional…it's our choice. We must get our souls so full of the Word of God (what God says about us), that the dragons' blast of fear-filled words through others and even through our own souls, loses its power. The words may very well be a fact, but we know the Truth, and the Truth has set us free. Fear verses Faith...fact verses Truth...darkness verses Light. The battles rage, but the Victory is already won.

I will be glad to leave this barren, parched wilderness behind me...won't you? There is one little problem...dragons travel. In the other kingdoms we will be traveling through, on our way to *a place called Peace,* you may feel the heat of a past encounter with a dragon. Or, as your eyes scan the horizon, you might detect smoke.

The really good news is dragons can be backed down. Their fear-filled hearts and the evil being of their master, dread the day we turn and face them with the *fire of faith* in our eyes. (Didn't someone say you can fight fire with fire?) When fear faces Faith, there is no contest. Any *princess* from the *realms of glory,* who knows who she is and whose soul has been renewed by the affirmations of her Father, can take on any fear-breathing dragon and watch him melt like a snowball in the hot August sun. That's *you,* Girlfriend...and that's *me.* Fear tolerated is faith contaminated, and we don't live there anymore.

So let us shake the ashes off our feet and move on...I think I see *Hope* up ahead.

Hope

Blackness abounds as I kick through
The rubble of my shattered dreams.
I see no future, only the darkness
Of my lonely past.
Then Father...in great Love
Picks up a fragment of my splintered self,
Perhaps the one called...Hope
And gently...with care begins to build
A new Life...a new Dream.
And this time nothing can shatter it
Because the foundation...is Him.

Assignments

THE KINGDOM OF FEAR

1. **Copy Second Timothy 1:7** *Up Close and Personal* into your journal:

   For Father did not give me a spirit of fear, but He has given me a spirit of power, of love, and a calm, well-balanced mind (soul)…full of discipline and self-control (paraphrased from the Amplified Bible, *Up Close and Personal*).

   Every time fear comes, read this Word.

2. **Make two columns in your journal. On one side write five of your biggest fears.** They can be current attacks from hell or the leftovers that burn into cinders every time they get heated up.

3. **On the other side of the column write five** *Up Close and Personal* Words from Scripture that contradict those lies. There is a Word of God for every single lie satan whispers to you.

   Reminder: The Word *Up Close and Personal* is taking a verse or passage from the Bible and paraphrasing it into your own way of speaking, putting your name and circumstances into it.

   Travel Tip: Most of the time you can find an alternative *Word* for satan's fear-filled lies in the Psalms. Just open your Bible and read Psalms until the Holy Spirit says, "That's it."

This is a tip for the *Bible beginners* among us. After a while, as you get more and more acquainted with the Word, you can find answers in every Book.

4. **Meditate on the Word of God that He has given you to replace the fear-filled lies.**

5. **Extend the time you spend** *practicing the presence* this week by five minutes.

   Every day this week for *fifteen minutes a day* get alone with Father. Write your conversations into your journal. Remember no topic is off-limits. He can handle it. He is shockproof.

6. **Record what you** *hear* **Him saying from out of your spirit. Write "Fear Tolerated Is Faith Contaminated"** in your journal ten times. Then write it in block letters and place it on your bathroom mirror. Read it often. Say it aloud often. (Remember, replacing fear with faith is labor intensive.) Although fear got us where we are, faith will get us where we ought to be. Rehearse the answer instead of the problem.

7. **What's your "fear factor"?** Pay close attention this week to where you tolerate fear. When you feel a dragon breathing down your neck, turn around and face him. Look fear in the eye and see it for what it really is…an assignment from hell to keep you from going forward into all God has for you.

In Case of an Emergency:

When fear sneaks upon you, or comes in on your blind side, speaking the name of Jesus will stop him in his tracks and pleading the blood will give him a major meltdown.

Example: If I begin to sense a fear from any direction about any area of my life, I say, "No! satan. This is not acceptable! In the name of Jesus Christ I command you to *go!* I plead the blood of Jesus over my spirit, soul, and body…over my children…my husband…finances… health… etc. (Include whatever area is under attack.) He can't cross the bloodline. If he tries, he's cosmic dust.

The Kingdom of Hope

THE SOUL'S ANCHOR

After passing through the dragon-filled *Kingdom of Fear,* this stop on our journey will be a refreshing change. The *Kingdom of Hope* is a cool mountain stream after a hot walk in a parched wilderness. So, for a little while, let's sit on this mossy rock under a shade tree, dangle our weary feet in the clean clear water, and talk about the motivation that keeps us going...*hope.*

The Word of God says that *"faith* is the substance [or title deed] of things *hoped* for..." (Hebrews 11:1 KJV). Before we can hold in our hand the title deed, or manifestation of our prayers, the element of *hope* must be present; therefore, this *kingdom* is a "must stop" on our journey.

As we get into the wonderful aspects of *hope,* we need to understand clearly the reasons Father created us with a soul. By now, some of us may be wondering if He really knew what He was doing, given all the trouble our souls have caused for Him and for us. Actually, He did.

When He created mankind as a spirit being, to have a soul and to live in a body, He intended all three elements to work in perfect unity. Our spirit, the real *us* was to be in charge, by being in constant contact with the spirit realm, that of course meant Him. Our souls (our minds, wills, and emotions) were to process into the world all the information we receive from Him. Our souls were never meant to run our lives simply because the soul is "user friendly" to a host of outside

81

influences, including satan. We are supposed to possess our souls, not the other way around.

(Our body always follows our soul. To the extent our spirit is in charge, it will flow with the Spirit...signs and wonders following. At the same time, to the extent that our souls have not been renewed by the Word of God and are still depending on natural reasoning, learned response, and negative core beliefs, our body will tag along and get us in more hot water than we can say grace over.)

The Holy Spirit explained it to me using some of the information most of us picked up by watching hours and hours of real-life television during the war with Iraq. He said that the Commander in Chief (our President) was at the top of all decisions in the war just as God the Father is at the top of our lives.

Central Command represented our human spirit with a resident General in charge, that of course, being the Holy Spirit. The Holy Spirit as the General in charge, gets His orders from the top...in our case, Father. (Remember, Jesus said that *He* [the Holy Spirit] *would tell us whatever He heard the Father say* (see John 14:10). Therefore *Central Command* is our human spirit, and all decisions should come from there. Only *General Holy Spirit* knows how our lives should be played out. Only He has *the plan* straight from the *Top*.

Our souls function as a *field commander* who passes the instructions on to the frontline troops. Nothing gets done if this part of the team is not receiving the messages. If communications are down, if he is so wounded he can't follow orders, or if he thinks he has a "better idea" than *Central Command,* the whole *plan* is in big trouble.

Likewise, if our soul is full of negative core beliefs, agendas, or wounds from the past, it too will be unable to carry out the *perfect plan* Father has laid out and related to the Holy Spirit. Because of its inability to hear the "orders," our soul will take up a defensive position and decide to fight the war all by itself. And that's the biggest problem in the Body of Christ today—renegade souls running lives and ministries when they have no idea what's in *the plan.*

Our bodies represent the *frontline troops.* Frontline troops in a war do just what they are told. They are *trained* and *equipped.* They are in excellent physical condition and are ready to do whatever it takes to carry out the orders from their *Commander in Chief.* Our bodies should function the same way. The only reason to be in excellent health and physical shape is to better carry out *the golden dream in the heart of God* for our individual lives. All we have to do is be the best we can be. God has the plan, and we're finding out that He's not trying to keep it a secret.

A Soul Set Free

Our soul is the creative center of our being. Our soul manifests our personality, the unique one-of-a-kind life force that makes each of us unlike any other being on the earth. It shows forth the attributes of our human spirit, which is the eternal part that gives the outward man personality. Our soul, in position to the input and leading of the Holy Spirit, enables us to become a gift to the world. It is our animated self. The soul is the database for an incredible amount of information. Even the most brilliant of us have yet to tap into the limits of a human soul or mind. A soul in the right position, merely implements orders; it does not generate them. The soul is the clearinghouse for every decision we make. We may not like it, but our everyday life is a direct result of what is in our souls (our core beliefs) and the decisions that have come out of those core beliefs. The revelation is that if we created it, we can re-create it, in the same way, using the power of our soul.

Properly focused, programmed, free from strongholds and negative core beliefs, we will see a soul set free. There is a no more beautiful, exciting, fascinating, productive thing upon the earth than a soul set free. A soul set free is a sign and a wonder. It's a sign of who we really are, and to the people around us, it's a wonder.

Not Everybody Celebrates a Soul Set Free

As we move toward *a place called Peace,* or wholeness, the people in our lives will be at a loss sometimes to figure us out. They will hardly recognize the "out-of-the-box" us. "What on earth has happened to them?" is a common response to the new and different way we are handling our life and them.

What happens? It is quite simple...the *hope* in our spirit begins to manifest in our soul and we become intolerant of our *present* and decide to create our *future.* We get tired of living on the edge of everything and decide to jump smack-dab in the middle and claim our best life. We get tired of "lack" and go after "more than enough."

Being tired of "almost," we leave. We may not have arrived yet...but we did leave.

We stop thinking, *I can't*, and begin to proclaim to the world, the universe, the angels in Heaven and all the demons in hell, "Yes, I can! And yes, I will! Furthermore, whatever any of you guys have to do to allow full access to the *plan of God* or me...get it done! Either get out of my way, or start bringing the resources to me, because *I will* walk out my *assignment* on this earth." And by the way, with these positive core beliefs in place and fully realized, nothing and nobody will be able to stop you or even slow you down. You will be walking in *the dream*, Girlfriend...with a *soul set free*.

Some days, you will be so full of this revelation that you won't even know yourself. Just who is that woman in the mirror whose eyes reflect the deep tranquil pools of peace in her soul and whose words radiate vision? Who is that full-of-confidence creature who walks into a room and her very presence demands respect? Although she can speak ever so softly, her laughter is spontaneous and full of joy. Who is that? She has an aura of *royalty* and yet at the same time love motivates her to "be all things to all people." Who on earth is that?

Answer: That's you and that's me. *That* is our *Father's daughter*...healed, whole, and free...right here on this earth.

Now multiply *that* woman by hundreds, and thousands, and millions, and you will see the *women of the glorious Church* walking out the *call of God* upon their lives before Jesus returns. These women will bring healing and wholeness wherever they turn. They will come from every walk of life and touch every social and economic level of society. We are on our way, girls, and the world is about to take notice.

As this transformation transpires, some of the onlookers will not fully appreciate the changes they see in you. There are a number of reasons, but all of them basically boil down to the fact that since you "got out of your box," "their box" is not as comfortable as it used to be. You're not predictable anymore. You seem just "too full of yourself" for their comfort. After all, up until now, your life had been *all about them*.

Their wounded souls can't count on you to react like you used to. Once upon a time they could set the climate for your day by just a word, but now no matter what "agenda" their wounded souls come up with, you just don't buy into it.

As much grief as they try to give you about the changes, they are also jealous. They wouldn't mind having your freedom, but the price you paid seems just too strange. (Getting up in the middle of the night to write words from Father in your journal...paraphrasing the Bible and putting your name in it... strange indeed.)

Since their own box is still a fortified stronghold, they sometimes hide in it and turn into "snipers." Snipers try to wound you just enough so you can be dragged back into the box they helped you create. You, back in your box, makes it easier for them to stay in their box. The thing we do if we are the least bit codependent is put our box inside their box so we can keep house for them. Makes things real handy...for them. Our best defense for the snipers in our lives is no defense. Nothing we can say will change anything for them. *They* are the deciding factor in their own lives, just as we were.

I remember as clearly as it were last week, the day one of my past personal snipers turned from aggressive to passive-aggressive and tried to hook me up one more time with feeling sorry for them. With tears they said, "Oh, I know I make your life miserable." My answer surprised even me. "No," I said in a calm clear voice. "No, you don't. My days of misery are over." And so they were.

I had better things to do than get back into that codependent box of trying to make *them* okay. *God had a plan* and I was determined to move my *hope* of walking in that *plan* into the *reality* of my everyday life. I had a mind to renew...I had a journey to take. And fooling around with what others thought about me was, as they say, wasting daylight.

An Owners Manual and Rules of the Road

Moving *hope* into the substance of *faith,* or *reality,* is the reason we have undertaken this *journey.* We want to be our best self, live our best life, and use our spirits, souls, and bodies for the glory of God. To accomplish this, Father has given us a personal manual to follow...an *Owner's Manual* full of *Rules of the Road.* He wrote it especially for us with our unique, one-of-a-kind *journey* in mind.

It is the Bible. Not the "historical book" the whole world knows about, but the *Words* from *my Father*, an *Up Close and Personal* Book talking directly to me. This is the further unveiling of Father's Plan B, after Adam messed up Plan A. This is the life that Jesus paid such a profoundly expensive price for....this is our future.

While we're resting by our mountain stream, in the *Kingdom of Hope*, let's get acquainted with our *Manual*. We need to be absolutely convinced that Creator Father, who designed and engineered the wonder that we are, knows how we work and how to fix us when we are broken. For the duration of this book and hopefully beyond, we are operating from a core belief that God, Almighty Creator of the universe and everything in it, had a specific reason for all of His creations.

It stands to reason, even Henry Ford created a car for a specific purpose. Likewise, Alexander Graham Bell created the telephone and many other inventions, all for a specific purpose. Therefore, how can it escape our notice that Almighty God might have had a specific reason for creating every single human being on the earth? He does, and it's all in *the Book*.

We, being *His number-one creation*, were given a first-rate handbook to explain how to keep the essence of who we are (our spirit, soul, and body) in tip-top condition. If that wasn't enough, Jesus sent the Holy Spirit as a personal tutor and guide. We have *the Book*...we have a *Tutor*...we have a *Guide*. Our part is to pick up the Book, ask the Tutor-Guide, who is living in our human spirit to help us, and make a *quality decision* to find quality answers. I believe you have made that decision. And once you become aware of how intimate and up-to-date the Bible is, your life will never be the same.

The Hope of Our Calling

Two of my favorite personal Words are found in Jeremiah 29 and Psalm 139. I literally copied these selected verses into my *peace journal* and placed my name in them. Yes, I know God was speaking in another time, in another place, and to a different people. But all prophecy is "divinely framed"; and because I know God to be my Father, I am in the "family picture" and I fit into the frame. What He said about His other children, He said about me. He is no respecter of persons, and He doesn't count time as we do. His timeframe begins before the foundations of the world and extends into eternity. I fit in there and so do you.

Read these Scriptures with me and insert your name.

*I know the plans I have for you, _____ , says Father, plans to prosper you and not to harm you... plans to give you **hope** and a future. When you, _____ , call on Me and come and talk to Me, I will listen to you. You have sought Me with all your heart and you have found Me...and I have brought you, _____ , out of the captivity of your past* (Jeremiah 29:11-14, paraphrased from the Amplified Bible, *Up Close and Personal*).

This clearly says He has a *plan* for us. This *plan* includes prosperity, safety, *hope* (there's that word again), and a future. He says that when we call to Him, He listens! He is saying, because we have searched for Him with our whole heart, He has been found by *us* and He has freed *us* from the prison house of our boxes. How cool is that?

Then there is the incomparable Psalm 139. No one knew better than King David the intimate detail in which God went to when He chose to involve Himself in the affairs of man. David knew *destiny* and he knew failure. He lived the history of all mankind as he experienced major victories and major "soul issues" at the same time. One day we find him as he is the celebrated one of Israel; another time he is pretending to be a madman running from his enemies.

Through all his ups and downs there is one thing we can say about David—he knew where to go for help. After every major mess-up we find him right back in *the Presence*, seeking God and asking for forgiveness. In Psalm 139 he is reaffirming what he knows to be the truth about God and His intimate knowledge of His children.

Listen as we read David's revelation paraphrased, *Up Close and Personal*.

O Father, You have searched me thoroughly and You know me. You know when I sit down and when I rise up: You understand my every thought. You sift and search out my every path... You even plan where I lie down. You are acquainted with all my ways. You even know what I'm going to say next! (I don't even know what I'm going to say next!) There is not a word in me that You don't already know. You hem me in, behind and before with angels (I am safe). You even laid Your hand upon my head in blessing...I cannot comprehend Your knowledge Father; it is too wonderful for me. There is no place I can go that Your Spirit wouldn't already be there. When I am in highest Heaven or in deepest hell, You are there for me. If I am flying on the wings of the morning as happy as a lark or spend time in a deep dark sea...even there shall Your hand lead me, and Your right hand holds me close. If I say "Woe is me, darkness is my only light"...even the darkness of my circumstances hides noth- ing...my darkness is light to You. You made all my intricate parts and knitted me together in my mother's womb. I thank You, Father! You planned me before my birth...what a wonder! Won- derful are Your works! My soul does magnify the Lord! Even my bones were not hidden from You when I was being formed in secret. Intricately and curiously You embroidered my features with the perfect colors for me in the secret place of mystery. Before my mother saw me Your eyes beheld my unformed body and You planned each day of my life before I was born! You even wrote "my plan" in a book.

O Father, how great are Your thoughts of me. How precious are the sum of them! I can't possibly count them. You think about me all the time! I could more likely try to count the sands of the sea until I fall asleep, and when I awoke (could I count to the end) You would still be thinking of me! And I would still be with You **(Psalm 139:1-18).**

What detail! What a plan! What a Father!

Even as I type this, my heart is beating faster in awe of how important each of *Father's daughters* are to Him. Think of all the girl babies ever conceived from the beginning of earth time. Think of the fact that He chose the details of their bodies...blond, brunette, tall, short, blue eyes, or brown...details, details, details...He was in the details and still is.

Think that before the sperm ever connected with the egg He had written a book with all the days of her life in it. Think of the reality that each one of them had an *assignment* upon the earth that only *they* could fulfill. Really stop and allow the truth to rush over your soul, that *you* are uniquely and wonderfully gifted to do what God has called you to do. He had it all planned before you were even thought of. He wrote it all in a book and set aside every single, minute thing you will ever need to take over your part of the *family business*. That includes all the finances, all the material goods, and all the *divine* hookups. Your *call* is even geographically located, and He knows how to get you there. The *Guide* to discovering all these wonders lives inside your human spirit...He is the Spirit of Almighty God! Talk about *quality leadership*. It don't get any better than this.

This is *your* journey in time. You have never been closer to your *destiny* than right now. Time dictates the hand of God upon you, and we have just read that He has put His hand upon your head. Now is your time. The anointing oil that Father has for you will not flow upon anybody else's head. It has been reserved especially for you. You were planned, ordained, and equipped.

Everything in your life heretofore has pushed you to this day. Every diabolical thing satan has ever thrown at you has been a vehicle to carry you to this place in time. He meant it for bad, but God caused it to become good. Your life-ministry is where your mess was...and Girlfriend, your life is just beginning.

Even as we *journey* on, the wonderful thing about this delight-ful *Kingdom of Hope* is that the memory of the calm, peaceful atmos-phere of our mossy rock by the mountain stream will be an anchor for our souls. The way may get rough...the dragons may show up... and the *reality of our faith* may be just down the road a piece, but *hope* is forever ours to keep.

If They Knew

What would people think
If they knew our secrets,
The secret tears we cry
The secret sins we hide?

What if people knew
The truth behind
The picture-perfect family
The picture-perfect dream?

What would happen
If I poured it all out
Into the streets
For all the world to see?

Assignments

THE KINGDOM OF HOPE

1. Note in your journal the things you personally *hope* to get out of this course of study.

2. Does the "chain of command" in the war analogy make sense to you? Are there core issues that may be stopping your soul (the field commander) from receiving clear orders from Central Command (the Holy Spirit)? If you can identify them, write them down.

3. This week add five more minutes to your time *practicing the presence. Each day* should include ten minutes for you to say whatever you want and ten minutes for Him to respond…twenty minutes total.

4. Do you recognize any "snipers" in your life? "By their fruit you shall know them."

NOTE ABOUT SNIPERS: Snipers can also hide in "religious boxes." We may go to a trusted *spiritual leader* about a situation in our life. We tell them all the terrible details of our victimized days and our nights of tears. They give us sound spiritual advice about not having to stay in an abusive relationship. So with their advice and encouragement, we take a step toward freedom. But then, something strange happens to our encourager—they backpedal and become snipers.

Perhaps another member of the family has gone to them and "complained" about the "advice" they gave. Maybe they become threatened that we really are getting drastic enough to "get out of our box" and the whole thing will put a serious dent in their own box. Whatever the case, they say something to the effect of, "Well...it is bad but don't get carried away. This is just gone too far...don't be hasty. After all, things could get worse." They are right—things could get worse and probably will...but we don't have to stick around to find out.

Beware of well-meaning but deceived people who undermine your decision to break unhealthy relationship patterns. *They can create self-doubt in you, and self-doubt can turn into self-sabotage.*

If you are a victim of any kind of physical, sexual, or emotional abuse, strategically disengage yourself long enough to get help. No woman on the earth should be treated like a second-class citizen. Father has a plan for your life and it does not include abuse. A decision should be made depending on the level of abuse. **Regarding any physical and or sexual abuse** against you or your children...**GET OUT.** Don't wait for more advice. Get yourself and your children (if applicable) and **GO.** You can fully expect Father to take care of you and lead you to safety. There are people to help you and the Holy Spirit will lead you to them.

Concerning emotional abuse: Abuse is defined as "to use wrongly or improperly...to mistreat or maltreat...to insult...to demean...disvalue... use course or insulting language...corrupt or improper practices." Quite frankly, it will depend on the individual state of our souls as to how we handle emotional abuse. A woman with a soul set free can stay in a relationship where emotional abuse *has been* present. I say "has been," because a woman who knows who she is, is not a candidate for abuse. The abuse may come out of somebody's mouth, but a "whole" woman can stand in the face of her abuser and say, "You may not talk to me like that. That is not acceptable behavior, and I will not put up with it." At that point, the abuser shuts up or the "whole" woman makes a quality decision about her next move. Because a "whole" woman has a personal relationship *Up Close and Personal* with Father, He will tell her exactly how to handle her individual problem.

To put it very plainly, a "whole woman" has no time to listen to lies and or somebody's "soulish" opinion of herself. She does not need their validation to know who she is. She has just talked to Father and His *opinion* is the *only* opinion that counts.

On the other hand, there are Christian women whose souls are so wounded by past and present abuse that staying in an ongoing emotionally abusive relationship is a form of suicide. She may be alive on the surface but her essence...the real woman...is simply gone. A woman in that situation needs to strategically disengage herself until she can have time to be healed and become whole. Sometimes living with ongoing constant emotional abuse is worse than physical abuse. Bodies heal relatively fast...souls can take years. If you find yourself in that situation, get free. Get some time for yourself to discover who you really are. Do this study course...go after peace...don't be afraid. Father is there to help you. Get to know Him. He loves you and thinks you are wonderful. You are...believe it.

5. **One Last Assignment:** Look in your Bible for a Scripture about *hope* that speaks to you. Write it in your journal *Up Close and Personal.*

   One of my favorites is Psalm 39:7: *"And now Father, for what do I wait for and expect? My **hope** and expectation for my future is in You, and I am safe."*

The Kingdom of Secrets

SO WHAT'S IN YOUR ATTIC?

To get to the *Peaceful Kingdom*, which by this time we realize is located in our souls, we must investigate even secret areas...areas that we would rather not go to ever again. They are just too cluttered...too old...too full of sad memories. Besides, what do they have to do with my new life? That was then...this is now. Right? Answer: True...and false.

True, we are to put the past behind us and we will, but a soul has a sneaky way of taking stowaways into its new territories. You don't know they are there until they jump out to cause trouble. So, take a deep breath; there is no getting out of this. We are about to take on a major housecleaning as we pass through the *Kingdom of Secrets*.

Out of the Attic

Years ago, Father gave me an idea to create dolls out of fabric and items most people would throw away. This idea came when my soul was in the depths of bondage, more than half full of negative core beliefs, unresolved issues, and an ache beyond words.

I gathered antique, vintage, and old fabric from the past and made one-of-a-kind dolls. I wrote an original story for each doll and attached it to that particular doll. Each story was different and yet the same. Each doll represented a woman or a young girl who had walked a troubled road full of challenges and hurt, into a life of wisdom and peace, a place I knew nothing about at the time. My spirit

95

was constantly crying out for *more*. So I created hundreds of dolls and wrote hundreds of stories. I sent them out into the world as a symbol of hope for women. I sent them out into the world as a prayer of hope for myself.

A marketing agent asked me if she could represent Out of the Attic Creations, and did so with surprising success. Somehow, these simple faceless dolls made from throwaways, caught the attention of women from all walks of life and in all parts of the country. In high-end shops and in galleries, Out of the Attic Dolls sat in quiet simplicity amidst expensive art and collectibles, drawing to themselves the very woman who would be touched by their attire and individual stories.

My agent did her job well and many Attic Ladies found homes to bless. In fact, Barbara Bush took a doll named Anna Grace back to the White House. I began to hear from women all over the country, who saw their lives in a different light after reading the story attached to a simple homespun doll.

One day I received a phone call from a lady in Colorado. She was a writer, author, and former editor of James Dobson's *Focus on the Family* magazine. She began to relate a familiar story. While on vacation, she had gone into a gallery and found a doll dressed in old fabric. The doll was wearing an apron made from a vintage print that reminded her of the dresses she wore as a little girl. On the apron was a tiny pocket and in the pocket were small treasures...like an antique button, a dried flower, a miniature pinecone gathered from a tree in the mountains of Kentucky. As I recall, these items were incorporated into the story.

Curiously, she picked up the doll and began to read, and as she read the story she started to weep. It dealt with a young girl taken from her beloved Kentucky mountains and moved to a distant place. It captured the loneliness a child can feel when she has no roots and everything familiar is gone. The tiny treasures in her pocket was all she had left of her childhood home. In the story, the yearning for a lost dream and a home had left a vacancy in her soul. I actually don't remember how the story ended. But it must have been a happy ending—all the endings were happy.

As my caller continued telling me her experience, I experienced a "God-is-in-the-details moment" myself. She said something to the effect, "The details in that story were almost a mirror image of what happened to me 30 years ago. I lived in the mountains of Kentucky, and when we moved, I lost something in that experience that my heart has been lonely for ever since." I could hear the emotion in her voice as she spoke, "I stood in that gallery and cried and cried. Something deep in my soul was so touched...I have no idea what happened. It was as though you knew what I had been through. It was all right there in the story. I knew I had to talk to you...you have touched my life."

It wasn't me that touched her life; it was Father reaching out to a wounded daughter by creating something beautiful out of her past. It was to be many years before I understood why Out of the Attic Creations was given to me to birth and bring forth into the world. It would be many more years before I "got it." In the meantime, I just wrote stories and made dolls.

Year after year, doll after doll, story after story the same "*God-is-in-the-details moment*" was trying to get a series of *realities* through to me. These *realities* included: In Father's eyes there are no throwaways. Nothing that happens to us is useless. It matters not if we have been discarded emotionally, or physically, by other people, or even by ourselves. He still creates beauty from the very things that have little value in the eyes of man. Not only that, as long as we are in the earth the "original story" can be walked out. You know the one...the story written by your *Creator* and attached to your life...the one where He planned every one of your days and worked out the details for your *assignment*...the story with the happy ending. O yeah...that story—it still belongs to you. (See Psalm 139 *Up Close and Personal* from last week.)

Every satanic attack in our life, every blind or stupid mistake we have ever made, every time we have failed God, our family, or ourselves, He can use to create a work of art. And just as Out of the Attic Dolls was created from the past and was able to touch many lives, likewise the *work of art* Father is creating from your past will be an instrument of healing to others.

Remember, your ministry is where your misery was. There are no disposable people, and it is never too late.

Cleaning House

In Philippians 3:13 we are told to *"Forget those things that are behind and press toward the mark of our high calling that is in Christ Jesus."* In one sense we, as Christians, are to forget those things that are behind. And for a long time I tried to just forget my past. I did not understand exactly what all "forgetting" entailed. Like multitudes of other Christians in the church today, I was taught it only meant, "Put your sins under the blood, and act like they never happen." That is a *true truth*. The blood of the Redeemer really has eliminated our past as far as God is concerned. When He looks at us, He sees only His perfect Son Jesus.

But I have learned that *forgetting* in the original language also means, "loose out of mind," or soul. In other words, *get it out of the attic*. We need to loose from our soul all past baggage and wounds, before we can press toward the mark of our *high calling*. The problem comes when we don't know what is in our attic, or soul. It may have been there for so long and had so much other stuff piled on top that we are unaware of how it has affected our mind, will, and emotions. We just aren't aware that an experience which happened 50 years ago is the cause of a problem we may have now.

When God gave me the idea for Out of the Attic Creations, He was sending to me, and to other women in the Body of Christ this message: It is time to get the hidden things out...the things placed there by our ancestors, society, and our bad choices. Clean them up...admit it was a stupid purchase...pray over them. Discard what is useless and create beauty out of what is left.

We are to clean out the attics of our souls, fill them with the fresh life-giving treasures of the Word of God, and allow the sweet wind of the Holy Spirit to blow through them, replacing death with life. Did you get that *we* part? *We* means you and me. If *we* don't take the responsibility for cleaning our house, it will never be cleaned. All the prayers prayed by every prayer chain we call will only bring us face-to-face with ourselves. *We* are the deciding factor. *We* create our lives from the inside out. For many years that was, for me, a really pitiful truth. I had a piled-up mess in my soul, and the life I had created reflected it perfectly.

Attic Dreams

God gave me two dreams that graphically illustrated the condition of my own attic. Having finally gotten free from the long-time tragic aftermath of a series of terrible decisions, I was trying to find some kind of serenity, forgiveness, and peace. Out of a pain-filled soul and not knowing how to find my way home, I had plunged myself and my children into unthinkable bondage. Because of the finely crafted plan of satan to steal my *assignment,* I had lost my dreams, my self-respect, and my confidence. I actually had lost custody of my life—myself.

Had I gone to the world system for counseling, I would have heard words like "victim mentality" and "codependent." In other words my self-esteem was so low that I had volunteered to stay in abusive situations and even enabled my abusers by covering up and pretending that everything was picture-perfect. All this took place after I had been saved more than 30 years. I had hit a brick wall and then I drove off the bridge.

My spirit (the real me) had continually reached out to Father. But my soul was so full of negative core beliefs that I couldn't hear Him speak. The voice in my spirit was faint and far away, unlike my soul which was a continuous roar of opinions, agendas, and issues.

As He has a way of doing, Father orchestrated a set of circumstances in which I, because of a sincere desire to "get fixed," was able to get myself physically out of the mess. Getting physically out of a mess was one thing...getting the mess out of me was another.

I had a new life, new people, new job, new car, new home, new geographical location, new clothes, new hairdo, new everything except a new soul. In the attic of my soul were years and years of accumulated, secretly hidden, and long forgotten wounds. These "soul issues" were continuing to clutter up the new life that Father was trying to make available for me.

The hidden hurt manifested in a number of ways. There would be times I would find myself weeping about the years of pain and suffering. I would weep about what might have been. I would weep for lost innocence. Sometimes I wept because I hurt. Such heart wrenching regret, soul sorrow, and remorse came over me when I thought of

the trauma I had inflicted upon my precious children by my decisions. I would feel sick physically and emotionally.

Yes, I had asked for forgiveness and I knew my past was under
the blood. Yes, I had asked my children to forgive me and had
received it graciously and in abundance. My children were strong
spirit-walking adults by this time, healed and in the ministry with
their wonderful mates. They were using the past pain to bring healing and wholeness to others. They were fine; I was the one with the
problem. New life...old me.

Then one early morning I had a vivid dream. I dreamed I had a
dead man in the attic of my new home. He was very old and very
dead. The stench of decay permeated the hot air in the attic. In my
dream the old man was seated in a wheelchair, and my sons were trying to help me get him down the stairs and out of the house. But when
we got to the door I said, "Wait a minute...let me see if anybody is
watching." I was very concerned that the neighbors would see us
removing the body. I didn't want the world to see what I had hidden
in my attic.

So, I closed the door on my sons, actually locking them up in
the attic with death, and went to see if my secret was being exposed
to the outside world. As I walked through my lovely new home
(new life), I could see coming through the air vents in the walls a
vile, sticky, putrid substance creeping onto my wall, polluting the
very air I breathed and defiling every lovely part of my house. And
then I woke up.

A few days later I dreamed I was lying in my beautiful new bedroom when a hole appeared in the ceiling. Out of the hole flew swarms
of flies and attached themselves to the walls of my room, leaving a
ghoulish, purple, oozing substance. I dreamed I jumped out of bed
and tried to wipe the effects of the flies away, but I couldn't keep up
with the spreading pollution. I grabbed a pair of jeans and tried to
stuff them in the hole to keep the flies in the attic, but it did no good.
They were there and they were destroying the beauty of my new life.
I woke up saying, "No satan! You cannot do this to me. Jesus, help
me...Jesus, help me."

It did not take a dream-interpreting expert like Daniel or Joseph
to help me understand the truth Father was trying to get across to me.

Something in the dark area of my soul was polluting my new life and would continue to pollute it as long as I kept it hidden.

It was also perfectly clear to me that my fear of what people would think and say was the reason I locked up the dead man. It did not escape my attention that a very old dead man in a wheelchair was quite helpless and could not hurt me. I was afraid of something that was completely harmless. He was affecting my life only because he was hidden, spreading his vileness through my otherwise lovely future.

In the dream, my sons stood for "my offspring" or in other words, the wonderful births Father wanted to bring forth in my new life, my part of the *golden dream in the heart of God*. They were locked up in an attic with death because I was afraid of what people would say. *The plan* was also locked up in the attic of my soul and was being polluted by a dead man who needed to be buried.

The second dream had basically the same meaning. What was hidden in my soul would continue to pollute my life until it was cleaned out. The jeans I had grabbed to stuff in the hole to keep the flies in the attic had a significant meaning. When we dream of specific items, they (most of the time) stand for other things, as in the parables of Jesus. (The sower went out to sow...the seed is the Word of God.) Jeans are pants, and pants stand for being in charge as in, "He wears the pants in the family." When I uselessly tried to stuff the pants in the hole to control the flies, I was being told that my soul was still "wearing the pants" and trying to control my life, but not doing a very good job of it. It didn't matter what I tried to do in the natural; the flies were there and they wouldn't stay hidden.

No matter how perfect I made my outward situation appear, there were things that had to come *out of the attic* before I could walk into my *peaceful kingdom*. About that time Father helped me take "soul searching" to a whole new level. The concept for this "map" you hold in your hands is one of the end results.

I began to see the truth and the truth, as it unfolded daily, began to set me free. Along the path of my personal *journey* I discovered some tools that could bring healing and wholeness to other women. As stated before, I do not consider this to be *the way*, but it is a way. It is a way that has been tested and tried and proven to be effective. It is the map Father laid out for me, and it is drawn in just the way He told me to draw it.

So, let us move on, into our week, and if we have to stop and ask directions every three miles, then so be it. Even if we haven't "arrived," at least we know we have left and that we are on the right road.

Forgiveness

You hurt me.
You took my last bit of dignity
And shredded it in my face,
Calling me names I can't repeat
And then you laughed at me.

You hurt my children,
Took their innocence away
And left a wounded soul
Where children used to play.
Then you said it was my fault.

Yes, you hurt me
But this day I am Healed.
I loose your hold upon my soul.
As I hand you Forgiveness
I walk away in Peace.

Assignments

THE KINGDOM OF SECRETS

Soul-searching

This week we are going to take our soul-searching a step deeper...as we go *back to the future*.

Back to our future simply means a segmented time travel into our past in order to clear the way to our future. This means housecleaning, and this is how it works:

1. **List your significant memories that happened between the ages of one and five, five and ten, ten and fifteen, and every five-year segment until your present age.** Write them in your journal as they are revealed. We will be working with this list next week.

2. **Answer the following questions as they apply under each entry:** How did I feel? Where were my parents when these things were taking place? Who cared about what was happening to me at this moment in time? Who was there making the brick that became a negative in my soul? Where was God when these things were happening? How do I feel about this situation now?

3. **Ask the Holy Spirit to help you recall things that might be significant.** Don't worry about missing something; it is the Holy Spirit's job to lead us into all the truth. As long as we are open, He can do His part.

Some Really Good Advice and a Warning

When you are ready to recall the incidents that may have impacted your life but are buried deep in your soul, do it when you are alone—just you, your journal, and the realization of the *presence* of the *Holy Spirit*. Ask Him to be there. Visualize Jesus and Father right there with you.

Please take a whole week to do your *back to the future* exercise. Do just one time segment a day. If the memory is just too devastating, *immediately ask* Father to help you—to hold you. He will…good Fathers do that. Please also remember that you have *the Comforter* inside you…at your service. No one *comforts* like the Holy Spirit.

P.S. Tears are okay…just call them liquid prayers.

Liquid Prayers and Healing Presence

This whole exercise reminds me of a story a pastor's wife told. She had noticed a young woman coming into their church one Sunday morning and sitting in the back with her head down. What touched her heart was the incredible sadness in her eyes. She had rarely witnessed such manifested hurt in one so young. Week after week she returned apparently beaten down by life, never smiling, never speaking. It was as though she lived in a cloud of misery. One day after the service, the pastor's wife touched her arm and said, "If you ever want to talk, I'm available for you." She did not expect her to respond, but the young woman called and set up an appointment.

Seated in the pastor's study, she poured out a story of devastating proportions. Her whole life, from the time she was born, had been one unimaginable tragedy after another. As she listened, the pastor's wife became overwhelmed with grief that a girl could suffer so much in one lifetime. She said all she could do was weep with the other woman as the details unfolded. She held her in her arms, and they wept and wept. As she finished, the pastor's wife began to pray in her heart, "O God, this is so terrible. I don't know what to say to her…I don't know what to do." Very quietly Father said, "Get her into *My Presence*, and I will take care of her."

She turned to the girl and said, "Okay, we're going to pray, and I want you to know that your loving heavenly Father is here. Just tell

Him everything you have just told me. Don't leave anything out. He is going to take care of it." She did...and He did.

Into the loving, healing hands of her heavenly Father she emptied her ravaged soul. Every sordid, diabolic, demon-inspired experience she had ever suffered she told to Father. And He was there to hold, and heal, and to make whole His broken child.

That day she stepped into her personal *Peaceful Kingdom* where nothing is missing and nothing is broken. That day she walked free from her past and walked into her future. She arose from that encounter with *the Healer* as *a daughter of royalty*, head high, a light in her eyes, a newness in her soul. The battered, beaten, depressed, victimized, pain-filled woman was no more. In her place was a powerful *woman of peace*, who went on to become a strong leader in that church and a joy to all who know her.

Father was there for her; He was there for me; and He will be there for you.

Back to Our Future Continues...

4. **As your soul gives up these memories,** you may feel once again that you are that little girl...or young teen...or whatever age you were when the incident took place. Do this assignment in the words of your age-level at the time. Let the "little girl" speak or the "young mother" or the "middle-aged woman." Hear her voice. Let her verbalize, perhaps for the first time, how these memories affected her. Embrace the strong overcomer she is. She has to be *strong* or else she would not have lasted this long.

Your list may look something like this:

One of the dominate memories I have between the ages of 6-10: I was six years old, and my little brother was three. We were living in a two-room apartment with Mom and our new stepdad. It was Christmastime. My brother and I got out of bed and sneaked into the kitchen where Mom had made lemon meringue pies. We ate all the meringue off the pies. Mom told our stepdad, and he beat us and beat us and beat us with his belt. What hurt most was Mom acting like it was okay, that we deserved every black and blue mark. What hurt most was Mom allowing it to happen. What hurt most was I had thought I was finally getting a daddy to love me. What hurt most was it was Christmas, and I was getting beat.

Questions:

How do I feel? Lonely...sad...hurt...guilty—my little brother didn't know better. It's my fault he is getting beat. I did it. Please Daddy, don't...I love you, Daddy...please don't...Mommy...Mommy, I'm sorry....

Who cares that my little brother and I are being beaten for eating the meringue off a pie? Nobody.

Where was God? I don't know. *In retrospect, I now know that God was there, loving us, but He limits His involvement in the decisions of man by giving him a free will. Out of wounded souls and demon-inspired actions, people can do unthinkable and unfair things to children. When I went back through this memory He was SO THERE. In fact, the only "leftover" from that painful memory is that I'm still not real fond of lemon meringue pie...but I do love to eat the crust out from under the filling!*

5. **Take your time. "Housecleaning" is hard work.** Stop every once in a while and have a cup of tea and celebrate yourself. You are becoming a "sign and a wonder."

6. **Add five more minutes to your** *practicing the presence* each day this week. That will be 25 minutes a day...every day. Just sit there, sip your tea, and let Him love you. Talk to Him in your journal. Let Him talk to you, giving Him equal time.

The Kingdom of Forgiveness

LETTING GO OF THE PAST

This *kingdom* is in actually a twin city with the *Kingdom of Secrets* that we explored last week. Situated as they are, side by side, we can't move on to *a place called Peace* without going through both of them, and learning the historical lessons each of them has to offer. So, let us take a moment to touch base with our *Guide,* the Holy Spirit and tell Him exactly what we want to see and do while we're here.

Dear Holy Spirit, thank You for giving us a guided tour of the kingdoms of our souls—the good ones as well as the really bad ones. Please show us as we pass through this kingdom of forgiveness how to move past, once and for all, the hidden secrets we discovered last week. Heal the hurts; heal the memories make us whole. Clear our spiritual perception of anything that is impairing our vision. We want to have eyes that see and ears that hear. Our one desire is to see clearly as You are leading and guiding us in the way we ought to go, and be able to hear Your voice as You counsel us, keeping Your eyes upon us. Thank You, Holy Spirit, for being our Guide on this trip. You are so welcome in our lives. You're the best...and we love You. Amen.

Back to the Future Revisited

The first time I sat down and did the exercise in last week's assignment of traveling back to my past in five-year segments, I experienced some very lonely pain. As I recorded the memories that were embedded in my soul and asked the pointed questions that pertained to the individual memories—how I felt at that moment…where were my parents…who cared…who was there making the brick that became a negative in my soul…where was God…and how do I feel now—it was almost too much to handle emotionally.

I did it in a six-hour continuous segment. (I don't recommend that you do that to yourself.) To experience some of this "sight-seeing," an hour a day is plenty and 30 minutes might be better. One of the reasons we have established weekly assignments and recommend the completion of only one chapter a week is to prevent the exploring of our souls from becoming too overwhelming. The best trips you will take have regular stops in order for you to regroup and refocus. Remember, the agreement *"My Commitment to Myself"* that you signed earlier stated that this course may raise issues, emotions, and truths that have been deeply buried for a very long time. Well, I know that to be the truth; it did for me.

My *back-to-the-future* moments revealed some very interesting *non-treasures* in the attic of my soul. When I did it a few years ago, I ended up having 10 segmented time entries. (Yes, that means I am over 50.)

The first three looked something like this:

Between the ages of 1 and 5: Violent father choking my mother…the little red rocking chair my grandpa bought me being smashed into splinters…having a nightmare of a freight train trying to run me down…waking from that dream and seeing my father standing over my crib screaming at me.

Between the ages of 5 and 10: Dad gone…Mom working day and night to support us…new stepdad…the "lemon meringue" deal…Mom gone off with new husband, leaving me and my little brother with grandpa…lonely—I miss my mommy…made up stories and told kids at school that my mom was a famous movie star—that's why she couldn't be with me…hated school—would have done anything to not go…rubbed poison ivy on my face so grandpa would think I had measles. (What I had was self-inflicted misery. I was very young when I started being good at that.)

Between the ages of 10 and 15: Back with Mom and step-dad...moving every two to three months...new schools...no friends...no roots...no "home" like other kids...lonely...step-dad following me around trying to get me alone...and did...Mom thinks it is my fault...is it?...still lonely...I feel dirty and guilty.

Well, you get the drift. And as the next seven segments and 35 years unfolded, it didn't get much better. Needless to say, my soul had its fair share of negative core beliefs. That is not to say I didn't have positive things deposited into my soul over the years also. Thank God, I did, or I wouldn't be here today with a soul set free. But it wasn't the "positives" that were cluttering up my life; it was the "negatives."

As you can see, I had some serious "housecleaning" to do. Some of these things had been in the attic of my soul so long they had cobwebs, dust bunnies, and layers of just plain dirt. Once I dragged them out to the light I asked Father, "Just what am I to do with this stuff?" He had a two-point answer: Number 1—forgive; Number 2—be thankful.

Number 1 was easy said, not so easy done...until I learned that *forgiveness* is a decision. It must be verbalized (because words create); it must be acted upon; and it must be done in faith. The way He led me into forgiveness will also work for you. But just as it has been with other stops on this trip, it may take a little time to get through this particular kingdom. The good news is, once you travel through this one, we only have six more to go!

Forgiveness 101

As I was wading through the debris in my soul not knowing how to "forgive and be thankful," I was blessed to have the *practicing of His presence* as a mainstay in my daily life. One day as I simply sat before Him, pen in hand, He led me to write down in my *journal* the present date and the names of every person involved with the deposit of "negative memory images."

He further instructed me to verbally—out loud so that my own ears could hear it—as well as on paper, *forgive*. I was not only to forgive them, I was to *thank them* for something positive they had given me, if any such thing existed. At first I thought that would be a real stretch for some of the folks on my list. But to my surprise, after I got the "stuff" out of the way, it was easier to remember happier moments and things to be thankful for. I discovered that few people are all bad. In fact, I personally have never known anyone who is "all bad." They are just people with problems...some worse than others.

I wrote:

To my biological dad: Dad, I this day, forgive you for hurting Mom...for embedding fear and anger into my young soul...for smashing my red rocking chair...for deserting us and causing Mom to have to work so hard. *Thank you, Dad*...for giving me life...for my introspective nature...for my inherited love for books and reading...for serving our country on the front lines during World War II...for bringing the bright pink paper parasol from Japan when you came home.

To my step-dad: Daddy, I this day, forgive you for not knowing how to discipline little children...for betraying the trust of an innocent little girl who just wanted a daddy to love her. *Thank you, Daddy*...for taking on a woman with two kids and doing your best to support us...for bringing my little brother and me candy and coke when you were courting Mom...for buying me new shoes when I started first grade when I didn't have any, before you were my daddy...for going to the parents of some big kids at school and stopping them from making fun of me...for becoming the man you needed to be before you went home to be with Jesus...for being a really good grandpa to my children.

To Mom: Mom, I this day, forgive you for deserting me physically and emotionally...for not knowing...for not understanding me...for not believing me...I know now you were only acting out of your own wounded soul. *Thank you, Mom*...for working so hard to support us...for giving birth to me...for my inherited creativity and the ability to "think outside the box"...for the times you taught us the games from your childhood and played with us...for helping fix up a playhouse for me when I was six...for the books you got for me...and the freedom to read them...for loving your grandbabies.

And on through the years I went, forgiving and being thankful. Not only did this exercise help clean out my soul from hidden and unresolved issues, it also helped me get a balanced perspective on my past. Not every image deposited into our souls by others are necessarily bad. It is just that the "bad" can hurt so much that we forget the "good." In addition, it is the twisted plan of the enemy of our souls to magnify the negatives until they hide the positives completely. Father's plan, on the other hand, is to *forgive and be thankful.*

This is a very powerful tool to use in our ongoing journey. When we write down our thoughts, we have a permanent record of our decision to forgive and when it takes place. At the time we make a quality decision to forgive, we may or may not *feel* like we have really forgiven. If the person is still alive, or even if he or she isn't, there may come a time when our soul has a flare-up and the old hurt comes back causing us to think, *I thought I had forgiven them. I must not have, because I feel hurt and angry again.* It is at this point you go to your journal, open to this exercise, and read. Read it out loud. Read it to your soul. Read it to satan. "It says right here, 'I, on this date, forgive...' " This was a *quality decision* from which there is no turning back, regardless of how we feel.

We, our spirits, the real us guided by the Holy Spirit, made that decision, and since we are the ones running the show now, *we* tell our mind, will, and emotions how they are to act. Our human spirits inhabited by the Holy Spirit can and should be in charge of our souls and bodies. *We* are the deciding factor, not a rebel soul who wants to hold on to the past just so satan can use it to beat us up. When one of those evil messages comes, write, "Wrong address" and send it right back were it came from. Just say, "Hello satan...you've got mail."

Forgiveness 102

I had made a quality decision to forgive everyone who had wounded my soul; but forgiving myself for having made decisions that had wounded the souls of my babies was another story entirely. I couldn't stop talking about my failure to my children. I felt such remorseful guilt.

Then one day my youngest son delivered a goodly dose of the "cold water ministry" for which my children are famous. "Cold water ministry" consists of a word of truth delivered so abruptly and in-your-face that the effect is like a bucket of cold icy water dumped over your head. This is a "reality check" in the finest sense of the word. This leaves the receiver blinking from shock. It is a word spoken in due season…or in my case, a past-due season.

There I was, *one more time*, going through my pitiful remorse of how my decisions had hurt the very people I loved most in the world. I happened to be on the phone with Chris when he stopped me in mid-litany and said, *"Mom, when are you ever going to let that go and stop talking about it? It's over…past…done! You need to move on!"* SPLASH!

There was dead silence on the phone while I caught my spiritual breath from the icy impact of my son's words. Then, "You're right, Chris…I'm sorry. From this day forward, you will never hear me talk about my past in guilt again." And I never did.

I had finally got it. He was right. Every time we replay a trauma in regret or pain, we reinforce it, giving it new life in our souls, adding color to the image, thereby giving it power over our present and our future. What we say with our mouths, our souls take as an order from the boss, even if it is a replay of an old record it already has on file. Our computer-soul takes what is programmed into it…good or bad. Our job is to remove dead files and key in new life-giving data. We are doing that very thing with our weekly assignments.

Well, we are halfway home. I don't know about you, but I'm feeling more and more ready to take on my part of *the family business*.

Almost There

A fragmented soul can fool you.
You speak the *Word* and it happens,

You ride on the glory of the moment

And even begin to think...I've got it.

Then your limits embrace you
And you are at a loss to know
What to do...what to say—
One fragment strong...another weak.

But for that one brief shining moment,
You were *almost* there.

Assignments

The Kingdom of Forgiveness

1. **List the people involved** in your "embedded image memory" exercise last week.

2. **Forgive and thank each of them in your journal.** Remember, you don't have to *feel* like doing it. It is a *quality decision* you need to make for *you*, not them.

   Note: An Option

   If the people are still alive and you know where they are, you have the option of going to them and forgiving in person. I personally do not think it is necessary...*unless* the Holy Spirit definitely leads you to do so. Sometimes they will react in a way that does not help a healing soul trying to get rid of negatives. My experience is you can receive healing and wholeness by just being in His presence, just you and Him. From that *place*, you can walk free. But, you are learning to be led by the Spirit, so just ask Him what the perfect plan is for you.

3. **By adding five minutes to your *practicing the presence*,** you will be spending 30 wonderful minutes a day, every day with Father. Do something a little different this week—try *practicing His presence* as you take a walk...read the Word... or drive in your car. Just *center* into your spirit and be so very aware of Him that *He* is the focus of your world, because you are the focus of His.

4. **Record in your journal how you feel about** *forgiving and being thankful.*

5. **FORGIVE YOURSELF!** Instead of focusing on the things you did wrong, record in your journal the things you have done right in your life. Yes, there are positive things to record. Look diligently...ask a friend...better yet ask Father.

For me it looks something like this:

I, this day, forgive myself for every mistake I made with my children. Father does not hold it against me; they do not hold it against me; I choose not to hold it against me.

I am thankful that all four of them are powerful men and women of God, in the ministry, and are raising families up to bring honor and glory to the Lord Jesus Christ.

I am thankful that all of my 12 grandchildren are prayed over every night and that their parents are teaching them to walk in the Spirit.

I am thankful that my firstborn granddaughter, from the time she was five years old, when asked what she was going to do when she grew up, would look you straight in the eye and say, "I'm going to raise the dead." (From day one she has been prepared to take her place in the endtime glory).

I am thankful that in a Mother's Day card I received this year my 30-something son wrote, "Thank you, Mom, for being the very best and awesome Mom in the whole world. Who I am and what I have done is because of you, your prayers, and faith in me...Love, Michael."

I am thankful that in the same card his beautiful wife and the mother of two of my "perfect" grandchildren wrote, "Thanks for making my husband for me, for your faith and prayers for me, and for being the best mother-in-law a girl could ever have...Love, Nicole."

How about that for positive affirmation? I believe I will dwell on these things. Paul tells us, *"Whatsoever things are lovely, whatsoever things are of good report...think on these things"* (Philippians 4:8 KJV). Well, I just believe I will! Sure beats the things I used to *think* upon.

Travel Tip

Even if we don't have any positive feedback from people, Father has provided a full supply. It's the *Word of God to His princess daughters,* and He always talks *Up Close and Personal.* Spend some time this week *dwelling* on the positives in your life. Write them in your journal. Read them to yourself especially when a "negative" pops up.

A Point of Interest

When peace comes to a woman, she gives birth to wholeness, and it will be manifested in her children.

Interlude

Before we continue on to the second half of our journey, let us stop for a few minutes and stretch our legs. Our *peace journal* has become a sort of travel diary, so let's compare notes and look at some of our souvenirs.

Notes From My Journal

Week One: The Kingdom of the Soul was a wake-up call. I need to "get out of the box, rethink, reexamine, and confront negative core beliefs. They have painted images of failure on my soul. They must be replaced with lovely images painted by the Holy Spirit.

Week Two: The Kingdom of Decisions made me *know* that if I want to change my life, it is entirely up to *me*. A *quality decision* is a decision from which there is no turning back, one I will sign my name to. My future is tied in the *holy moments* of my daily decisions. I will get out of life only what I am willing to go after.

Week Three: The Kingdom of Fear is where satan's dragons live. I found out exactly where and how satan finds a place to cause damage to me, how he plants the seed of fear, and how I bring it to pass by meditating on his lies. If I tolerate fear, it will contaminate my faith. I have power to rebuke satan. Jesus came to set the captives free…and *I am free!*

Week Four: The Kingdom of Hope gave me just that…*hope*. I have *hope* for my soul and *hope* for my future. God has a wonderful plan for *my* life, and I mean to find out what it is. I see the light at the end of the tunnel. I learned about "snipers" who are hiding in their own boxes waiting to take a shot at me. I make them uncomfortable, but I also found out it is all right if others do not understand the changes taking place in me. Father likes me "out of the box." I am a *princess in the realm of glory*, and I am a force upon the earth.

Week Five: The Kingdom of Secrets really did take soul-searching to a whole new level. I feel I deserve a *"Good Housekeeping Seal of Approval"* for the thorough job I did in the attic of my soul. I had no idea that the images painted by people in my past dictated my future in such a graphic way. It's like getting terribly burned. It can happen in a moment, and hurt for a long, long time...but the scar can last a lifetime. My soul had been scarred and disfigured. Long after I had hidden the pain in the attic of my soul and it had stopped hurting, the scars still affected me. I have to come *out of the attic* before I will ever find *a place called Peace*.

Week Six: The Kingdom of Forgiveness actually made sense to me. I am not forgiving them for *them*; I am forgiving them for *me*. I deserve to walk free from the past. I refuse to harbor anger, guilt, hidden pain, rejection. No one is "all bad." Every single wounded soul who had a hand in the negative images embedded in me also left lovely images as well. *I thank them with my whole heart for the roses they gave to me, the laughter, the fun, the nice things, the good times...I truly am grateful.*

How wonderful it was to learn how to forgive myself.

I can see peace up ahead!

Discovery

The negative things I as an adult experienced from people would not have been so traumatic for me *if* I had not had so many "soul issues" of my own. Yes, they may have had problems, but *my* real problem was *me*. Knowing what I do now about who I am in Christ Jesus would have stopped any abuse in its tracks. There comes a time when we are no longer "victims" and we become "volunteers." And I don't live there anymore.

Checkup

Spend some time going over the entries in your own *peace journal* for the last six weeks. Are there any assignments you need to go back and do? Remember this whole *journey* is based on "getting to the other side" of the *kingdoms of our soul*. If we detour around a particular kingdom, we will never know what it contains or provides. We won't know who lives there or how the information we pick up there will help us on our continuing *journey*.

Joyce Meyer says that with God, we never fail a test; we just keep taking it over and over until we pass. A missed detail in our *journey* means our progress is slowed down considerably. And until we know the *truths* to be had in each *kingdom,* we will be susceptible to a deception. *God is in the details...don't miss any.*

Halfway Home

We are halfway to *a place called Peace*. We understand more about ourselves, our past, and how satan has used it against us. We fully realize that we are a spirit; we have a soul; and we live in a body. We also know which one has the tendency to be a rebel and must be tamed.

Our soul is the conduit for our lives. Everything we see in the natural realm has to come through a human soul. Our personal lives are a reflection of what is in our personal soul. Our bodies, being followers, show, look, act out exactly what is resident in our souls...for good or bad. A soul unrenewed by the Word of God (which is perfect love), will simply create a life with what it has to work with...the images embedded in its core.

Our human spirits, the real *us,* are supposed to be the origin of our daily lives. The majestic Holy Spirit lives inside our human spirit for the sole purpose of helping us walk out the *golden dream in the heart of God* for each of us. The *dream* is in us. He is in us; therefore, Heaven is in us. But it must be processed through our souls and implemented through our bodies. That's how we get *days of Heaven on earth.*

As we have dutifully spent the last six weeks completing the readings and assignments, meditating the Word *Up Close and Personal,* and spending time *practicing His presence,* our souls have been impacted. We have experienced healing in many damaged areas of our souls as these daily impartations of *truth* were meditated upon. They are now being acted out by our bodies to re-create our lives. That's how the system works. That's the only way it works.

Jesus says in Matthew 5:48, "*Therefore ye shall be* **perfect** *just as your heavenly Father is* **perfect** (emphasis added). This does not mean sinless perfection. Young's Concordance says the word *perfect* used here is "the ability to repair and adjust." We are learning to "repair and adjust." It's also called *spiritual maturity*.

Secrets of the Morning Pages

For the next six weeks, we are going to add a new and surprisingly effective tool to our "exposing the soul" toolkit. It is called the *morning pages*. It is simply three pages of long handwriting first thing in the morning. They don't have to make sense...or make anything. They simply are three pages of the first thing that goes through your mind when you wake up in the morning. That's it. Period.

Morning pages do a number of things. First, through the pages, satan's hidden agendas are revealed. All the tiny seeds of doubt, negativism, hidden pain, and questions appear on the *morning pages*. They clear the slate of all the petty, whiney, aggravating things we carry around in our souls. *Morning pages* expose them for what they really are...petty, whiney, and aggravating. They serve as a visual conscious—the gauge for the state of our souls. They get us moving from Point A to Point B. For instance, we can't whine over and over, day after day, about an obstacle to our moving forward, without doing something about it.

Once it hits the *morning pages*, it is sitting in the light...no longer hidden. Whenever we see an obstacle, our born-again spirit wants to do something about it. That's when *the Helper* gets involved. This is yet another dimension of "*You shall know the truth and the truth will set you free.*"

Example: If I were to write in my *morning pages* day after day, week after week, about those last 10 pounds I need to drop, the closet and drawers that need cleaning, the curtains that need washing, the fact that I drink too much coffee or watch too much TV, *I*, the real *me*, my spirit would get tired of all that soulish stuff and call for a *quality decision* to DO SOMETHING!

Morning pages get us centered. They move debris out of our souls onto the page so that we can more clearly receive the Holy Spirit's inspired plans and purposes. We don't have to *think* about *morning pages*. We just drag ourselves out of bed onto the pages, getting up a half hour earlier if we need to. No one said renewing a mind was easy. What we did say was, it is mandatory if we want to be part of the *glorious endtime Church*, full of the power and grace of God. What we really *know* by now is, *if we want to get to where we have never been, we're going to have to do something we have never done. Morning pages* are possibly something you have never done.

When I began *morning pages* on a consistent basis less than a year ago, I was rather skeptical. I did it out of the leading of the still small voice in my spirit. I had journeyed far enough along in my *Peaceful Kingdom* to be enjoying peace more often than not. I already knew the basic concepts I am sharing with you, but I lacked definite direction about my next step. I just had this inner knowing that this would help me to sort myself out…into what I didn't know. So every morning, I would get up early and write three pages of anything.

I really did not know until a few weeks ago that I was performing a daily housekeeping of my soul. All I knew was that every morning I would write whatever came across my mind as soon as I woke up. Some of it was pretty petty. Actually, a lot of it was petty at first.

For instance:

What am I supposed to do today? There is a pain in my left leg— what is that about? All grace, every favor, and earthly blessing come to me from Father in abundance. I have need of nothing. I need to go to the gym three times this week, but all I can think about right now is a cup of Starbucks coffee and a sticky bun. Why did they build a bakery so close to the gym? I have joy, peace, love. I need to wash all the curtains in the house. The linen closet is a mess…order…order…order. I am a happy woman. Pain radiating down my arm to my leg. Wonder why Lisa hasn't called this week…what's up? These pages don't make sense. Lots of non-stuff….(and on and on).

Who would have thought a mind could be so cluttered so early in the day? Putting all that on paper got it out of my soul and therefore off my mind. I was relieved as I went along that more and more Word was flowing out of my soul daily. Sometimes a weird thought, like doubt and unbelief, would flow out, and I knew that lucifer was up to something. But more and more, a direct leading from the Holy Spirit would emerge from my spirit into my soul and onto the *morning pages*. Daily exposing any and all false data, the lies of satan, and your own soul's agendas gives your spirit a chance to do something about it. *Morning pages* are a big-time exposé.

One possible hindrance to getting real on the *morning pages* is that some of us have been rightly taught not to talk negative. We have been told, "You get what you say...don't allow negatives to come out of your mouth...words create." True, true, and true. *Morning pages* do not come out of your mouth; they come straight out of your soul. As we, for sure know by now, our computer-soul can store junk as well as treasures. Don't be afraid to put down the seeds of fear satan has dropped on you. Write anything on the page. Write three pages of it on the page.

They are an excellent guide to how much Word your soul can activate at any given moment. *Morning pages* locate us. We get real about what is truly in us and what is trying to manifest through us— anger...frustration...exhaustion.... They are also a wonderful barometer of our receptivity to the leading of the Holy Spirit.

The results of this discipline astounded me. I went into it half-heartedly, thinking maybe I would write a page and a half. Although I knew I needed to do them, I wanted to compromise. But after six weeks of getting up a little earlier and day after day of writing three pages of whatever, this book emerged.

I remember as I wrote my usual pages of "not much," *The Search for Peace* began to flow straight from the Holy Spirit, through my cleaned-out soul, onto the pages. I wrote and wrote and wrote. It was almost as if I was taking dictation. I was amazed, astounded, and downright humbled. Whole chapters of *'The Search'* sprang full blown onto the *morning pages*. It was so exciting that I couldn't wait to get up in the morning to see what He would say next. Four a.m. seemed to be His most prolific time, but what did it matter? It didn't. I wrote the first draft of this book in six weeks...early in the morning...on the pages.

Up until that time, I had not written for publication for 20 years. During those 20 years, I was living the life which you have seen in snapshots throughout this book. I had worked for years at *practicing the presence*, meditating the Word *Up Close and Personal*, and journaling. *Morning pages* was the final discipline that moved me into my personal *assignment, call, destiny*.

By this time, it wasn't the big problems I had to overcome; and as you can tell, there had been some *big ones* hindering my forward velocity. After all the major soul problems had been healed and rectified, and truly placed in the past, it was the daily clutter that needed to be cleaned. *Morning pages* did that very thing.

When we shared this tool with the Women of Peace, the ones who took it seriously had the same amazing results. One of the ladies discovered as I did that once you get all the "stuff" out, the Holy Spirit can begin to flow onto the page. She was writing along, mostly complaining about not having a job, not having direction, just not having. "What do You want me to do? I'm tired of this," etc. etc. When all of a sudden, she saw these words flowing from her pen: "I want you to open a Christian bookstore." He told her where to locate it, how much rent to pay, what to name it, and who was supposed to help her.

When she went to *the place* designated and talked to the person in charge, guess what? The *rent* asked was exactly to the penny, the amount that had flowed onto the page. Needless to say, this *morning pages* devotee can hardly wait for morning to come to see "the rest of the story." All of us have heard that when God guides, He provides. We're finding that to be true in the finest sense of the word. There is no lack in the Kingdom of Peace.

One wonderful thing that happens after the first few days of writing is that *morning pages* turn into *pages in His presence*. They become a conversation with Father, a form of meditation…a quiet time…a centering…a tangible way to hear His voice. When this happens, just go with it. Write all the "stuff" from your soul. Write your prayers for your family. Write the petty distractions that satan will no doubt drop into your mind to deter you. Write it all.

By writing even the distractions that satan has planned to use to get you away from the pages, you can give him an Excedrin moment. For instance, you are flowing along writing about how wonderful it is that the blood of Jesus covers you and your family, "Glory be to God—Father, I love You," when out of nowhere comes the thought, "Better go see what that dog is barking at. The laundry needs to be done now. Did you unplug the iron last night?"—all satanic bulletins to get you away from the pages. Just keep writing. Write his messages…and carry on with the praise and thanksgiving to God. Just write and don't quit. Your future is inside you. It needs to flow out, and it can do that on the *morning pages.*

A Decision of Quality

So for the next six weeks as we complete our *Search for Peace,* just make yourself do the *morning pages.* There is no way to do them wrong. If all you write is "This is stupid…I wish I were in bed," then fill the page. Just fill the page. Don't reread your thoughts for six weeks. Don't share them with anybody. Don't contemplate or analyze what you are writing. Just write.

A Word From Father about the Morning Pages

Remember His analogy about our spirit using our soul the same way our body uses our brain. At the same time, He had this to say about morning pages:

*One of the most important assignments is the **morning pages.** **Morning pages** are like x-rays of a damaged brain; large gray areas of your soul become visible on the pages. X-rays show where the problem lies, as well as healthy tissue. **Morning pages** do the same.*

Only the fully functioning part of your soul is open to My leading. A soul (mind, will, and emotions) that has shut down puts the human spirit in a coma of sorts, just as a physical brain that shuts down puts the body in a coma. Too many of My people are in a coma, shut down by a traumatized and wounded soul. I want them free.

Postscript

Because I had diligently emptied my soul every morning onto the pages, there was a free flow of the Holy Spirit inspiration. He was able to show me the *golden dream in the heart of God* for me. If you will diligently follow the disciplines laid out in this book, that time will come when you too will discover the *call, the destiny, the asssignment* for the *authentic* you. You will see with eyes that see and hear with ears that hear. You will have arrived at a *place called Peace.*

The Kingdom of Partial Peace

A FRAGMENTED SOUL

This *kingdom* fools you because it looks so much like the *Kingdom of Peace*...if you don't look too close. Truth be told, we got here exactly the way we get to the *Peaceful Kingdom*...almost.

When you are at *partial peace*, you are almost there. Parts of your soul's negative core beliefs have been replaced with positive core beliefs, and from the positive foundation part, wonderful things transpire. It is also quite possible that a positive core belief can be programmed into us from childhood. Therefore, when we accept Jesus as our personal Savior, we are immediately able to excel in one area where our faith is strong. This is the case when you see a Christian, figuratively speaking, "walking on water" in one area of his soul and be a total train wreck in another. That was me.

As a child, I cannot remember not believing in divine healing. I knew God healed, and if He had to do a supernatural miracle to accomplish the act, then so be it. I cut my spiritual teeth on stories about miracles, such as the story about Aunt May.

Aunt May was my grandpa's sister and my great-aunt. As a young woman, she was diagnosed with cancer. In the 1930's medical science was naturally not as advanced as it is today, and when they operated on Aunt May, hoping to remove the cancer from her abdomen, they found it was too far gone. There was almost nothing left—no uterus, no stomach, no ovaries—everything had been consumed by the cancer. The story goes that they packed the cavity with cotton, sewed her up, and sent her home to die.

My grandpa was a hellfire and brimstone preacher and a coal miner in the West Virginia mountains. As far as I can tell, he knew little about the gifts of the Spirit; all he preached was, "If you don't get saved, you will burn in hell," and evidently he knew God could heal. When they sent his sister home to die, they called him out of the mines to pray for her.

Covered with coal dust, he walked into that little bedroom, his blue eyes glaring out of his blackened face. Evidently, the gift of faith or healing came upon him, because he laid his hand on her and commanded that cancer to leave her...and it did. Aunt May arose off her deathbed and was so completely healed that in the years to come she conceived and had a baby girl. God had completely re-created her reproductive organs.

Having been raised on this *reality*, I could never be swayed from this truth, not by satan nor by my fragmented soul. Consequently, when I married and began to have a family, I told them the stories, and I lived every day of their lives fully expecting God to take care of my children with miracles if need be.

Along with that positive core belief firmly embedded into my soul, I added to my "child protection arsenal" by meditating on Isaiah 54:13-17: "My children are taught of the Lord and great is the peace and the undisturbed composure of my children...and no weapon formed against my children shall prosper."

Therefore, when satan, or their own carelessness put them in harm's way, I fully expected God to do whatever it took to "fix my kid," and "fix my kid" He did. I saw His healing miracle power in everything from a tiny three-year-old finger cut to the bone, close up before my very eyes at the name of Jesus, to a terrible accident that could have taken my son's life.

I was living in Kentucky and my youngest son, who was about 18, had moved to Texas to work for his brother. He was framing houses and was on top of a two-story house working when something happened and he fell two stories headfirst onto the concrete foundation. His brother immediately called me on his cell phone and said, "Mom, Chris just fell...it looks real bad...." Even as he spoke, I was aware of my reaction; I got quiet inside and began to have a conversation with Father.

The hours I had *practiced His presence*, my childhood "programming" about miracles, and the Word of God about my children that I had meditated on over the years, all came together. I was aware that I was *centered*. I shut out all the negative facts I was hearing my son relate and listened to the Holy Spirit residing in my spirit. And we had this conversation:

Me: "Okay, Father, what is this?"

Father: "Satan is trying to take his life."

Me: "Father, this is not acceptable. That boy belongs to You and to me. Satan has no right to him."

All of this took place in a split second. It doesn't take long to do business with Heaven when you know Heaven is inside you. At a time like this, under the pressure of an attack from hell, the first words out of our mouths will locate us, clearly showing what is in that area of our souls.

So, to my son I said, "Okay, here's the deal. Take him to the hospital and do whatever the doctor says to do. But let me tell you one thing—CHRIS WILL WALK OUT OF THAT EMERGENCY ROOM THIS DAY COMPLETELY HEALED! DO YOU UNDERSTAND ME? THIS DAY. YOU SPEAK LIFE TO HIM. THIS DAY HE WILL WALK OUT!

By that time my faith was manifesting itself loud and clear. My voice held an authority beyond a mother's authority. It was the power of Almighty God roaring out of my spirit, validated by the area of my soul that knew it to be the truth, and my body (mouth) was speaking creative power that manifested a thousand miles away in the body of my child. At that moment my spirit, soul, and body was in perfect synchronicity.

On the phone I heard Chris's brother catch his breath and say, "Okay...." I hung up and ripped into satan telling him *who* I was, *who* my son was, and demanding, "Just *who* do you think you are?" Then I told him *what* he was in no uncertain terms. I spoke *LIFE* to Chris. I spoke death to satan's agenda. Then I began to laugh at the devil for having the audacity to touch my child. I told him he had really stepped over the line this time, and he was in a world of hurt because *this day* the power of God would be manifested.

I gave them enough time to get to the hospital, and then I called the emergency room. I told them who I was and requested to speak to someone who came in with Chris. When his brother answered, I asked, "Okay...what's up?" He laughed and said, "Here, ask him yourself." The next voice I heard was Chris's Texas drawl.

"Hi, Mommy."

"Chris, what have you done?"

"Well, I reckon I fell on the hardest part of me."

That day Chris walked out of the hospital healed.

Fragmented

In that area, my soul (my mind, will, and emotions) had been renewed to the *Truth* of the Word of God. *Truth* overcame and manifested itself in the face of a natural fact. The fact was Chris was gravely hurt and could have died. The *Truth* was what I knew the Word of God said: "*No weapon formed against my child can prosper....My children are taught of the Lord and great is the **peace** (nothing missing...nothing broken) of my children.*" In that one area of my soul, I knew who I was and I knew my position in Christ Jesus—in *that* one area.

At the very same time, in other areas of my soul where "my programming" and lack of Word had created negative core beliefs, I was an accident looking for a place to happen. At *the very same time,* I was still a passive-aggressive control freak, a codependent victim, and I suffered from a number of deceptions such as bulimia and was at times paralyzed by insecurities...at the very same time that I had spoken a miracle into my son's life.

The Kingdom of Partial Peace can be deceiving. Given enough areas of positive core beliefs and given enough victories coming from the areas of soul renewal, you and the others in the vehicle with you will think you have arrived at *a place called Peace.* Not yet. It looks like it; God is clearly at work in your life; signs and wonders follow—but not yet.

This is where we have to pay closer attention to the scenery around us. We have to see the weeds as well as the flowers. This is where we have to become brutally honest about the rest of our lives. This is where we have to ask the Holy Spirit to manifest Himself as a *revealer,* showing us exactly what is in our souls. This is where we must work diligently to reprogram all past negative wounds with the Word of God that specifically applies to them.

It is this ability of a soul to be partially renewed that confuses and brings reproach upon the Body of Christ today. We see "leaders" having wonderful authentic manifestations of God in their ministries, while their personal lives leave much, much, much to be desired. (That is putting it kindly.) One well-known minister was a little bit more candid. He said, "They pull fire down from Heaven and have the morals of an alley cat." What they have is a fragmented soul, some parts good, some parts not so good. They dwell, set up residence, and abide in *the kingdom of partial peace.*

That is not an option for us. *Partial peace* is a breeding ground for *deception.* (We will discover next week more about that devastating *kingdom.*) But we can't afford to settle for *partial* when we are headed for the *golden dream in the heart of God.* We must *"lay aside every weight, and the sin that so easily beset us, and let us run with patience the race that is set before us"* **(Hebrews 12:1 KJV),** because as the poet has reminded us, "We have miles to go before we sleep."

Deceived

It comes as an angel of light,
A spark dropped into the darkness of our lives,
A voice soothing…soft…persuasive.
We take his words depositing them one by one
Into our wounded past creating a false hope.
Blindness sets in as the evil is developed.

It begins in our ear then slowly moves inside
As it is meditated into our fragmented souls.
The angel of light whispers to us,
"He sent me…He wants this for you…it's okay."
We don't know he is a messenger sent
From the evil prince of the damned.

We don't see that his shining robe of light
Is only a cover for a shroud of darkest death.
We don't see the inferno blazing in his eyes
Nor detect his fiendish grin when he turns away,
As we willing step forth in deception
At his bidding and do the unthinkable.

Assignments

THE KINGDOM OF PARTIAL PEACE

1. **Are there areas in your soul you can recognize as not being right?**

   For instance:

   You have undeniable gifts of the Holy Spirit working in your life, yet depression lays on you like a heavy cloak. Or you can't seem to stop doing something your spirit knows is wrong.

   You pray for the sick and they are healed, but you can't maintain your own healing.

   You are a beloved Sunday school teacher, but at home you scream at your own precious children like a woman possessed. (p.s.—You are not possessed.)

   Record any areas you know you need help with...allow the Holy Spirit to reveal others.

2. **Regarding the areas of your soul that need renewing, find Scripture to help you with that process.** Remember it is a "process." (This is the end of the quick fix, but the payoff for diligence is so fine!)

3. **You are spending 30 minutes a day *every day* with Father.** If you haven't already, add a few minutes more... say five.

4. **This week, begin writing your *morning pages*.** First thing every morning, write three pages of anything. It matters not what is written on the page. You are emptying your soul of possible hindrances and also finding out about the good things already embedded there. Meditate (roll over in your mind) the *fact* that Father has a wonderful *plan* for your life, and it just might appear on your *morning pages*.

A Reminder: *Morning pages* **are a form of prayer; use them as such.** As you are diligently writing *whatever*—a prayer request, a thought about your children or mate, Scripture—write it. Write anything and everything that crosses your mind in the morning...even distractions from satan. If they are on the page, they are off your mind and out of your soul.

Postscript: Remember my son Chris who did the high dive off the top of the house? A short time after he had walked out of the emergency room healed, he was changing the letters on a sign possibly 20 or more feet up in the air. He was working alone, and sure enough he fell. He said he was praying in the Spirit before he hit the ground.

Laying there apparently paralyzed but conscious, he began to talk the Word. Before long, all feeling came back, and my boy climbed back up into his high perch and finished his job. I can't say I was surprised...it's a family tradition. Father takes care of my kids. We expect miracles.

Chris is now passing on the family tradition of trusting God to his beautiful daughter. Who could have guessed that when a little West Virginia mountain girl was told over and over the miracle story of Aunt May, a half century later that positive core belief would insure that a little Texas angel with golden hair, named Amie Lynne, would be born and call me Grandma? *Father is so good.*

The Kingdom of Deception

A LAND OF DENSE FOG

The *Kingdom of Deception* is a treacherous land of dense fog. The farther we travel into it, the less visibility we are afforded. We become disoriented and confused, and if we don't get out of it soon, it will destroy us as well as the people in our lives we love the most. The fog only makes the danger of the sinkholes full of quicksand even more deadly. Once you step into one, it tends to swallow your life. The evil prince of darkness loves this territory. It is the one he brought with him into Eden. It is the one he daily invites the Body of Christ to inhabit.

The Unthinkable

It is 4 a.m. and a full hazy moon lights up the desert landscape outside my West Texas home. Hundreds of miles east of me, the same moon lights up the sky where two little brothers will be soon laid to rest.

Something terrible happened to their mother. A few hours before Mother's Day, she took them out of their beds into their backyard and beat them to death with rocks. Then she took a rock inside to where her 14-month-old baby slept. When she was done, she covered him with a pillow and calmly called 911 on her cell phone and said, "I've killed my children."

When the police arrived, they rang the doorbell waking up the sleeping father. He told the police they had the wrong house. But in the backyard was a mother covered with blood. Two of her babies were dead, and another lay bleeding near death in his crib. And the demons in hell danced with glee, because another of God's children had been deceived.

It is 4 a.m. and my heart is being poured out in prayer for that family, the church where she was active and where her brother-in-law pastors, the community, and most of all for that mother. Reports say she alternates between curling up in a fetal position and sobbing for her babies, and calmly speaking the Word of God and praying. She says, "I had a vision and God told me to do it."

I don't know her; my son and his wife do. They have met her and are friends with some people in her church. She appeared to be a wonderful, gifted woman of God—everything a Christian mother should be—the perfect person to leave your child with for the afternoon. Church members were frequent visitors to her lovely home, a home that once rang with the happy noise of little boys' laughter but now sets empty...a designated crime scene.

O Father, whatever it takes, open the eyes of Your Church. Give us ears to hear. Teach us to know the difference between words from Heaven and words from hell. Move us from religion to reality. Help us to stop playing church, and renew our minds until we get so sensitive to the voice of Your Spirit that nothing like this ever happens in Your Body again. Wake up the Church in this land, Father! Have mercy on Your people. Lord, we need help.

Harvest of Death

No one can say for sure how this tragedy began or what lie satan first planted into this mother's soul. But somehow a seed was planted, taken, and brought forth fruit. That's the way it works. For good or bad, it all begins with a thought...a seed. The fall of man began with a thought planted into Eve's mind when satan said, "Did God really say...?" Eve entertained the thought and then acted upon it, resulting in spiritual death for all mankind.

Four thousand years later, satan came to plant thoughts into the mind of Jesus in the wilderness. That is his mode of operation. Thoughts planted by satan into the soil of a wounded soul or unrenewed mind can still bring forth death. He doesn't have any new tricks, but he has practiced this one until he has it down to a fine art.

And every day, in small insignificant ways and in huge tragic ways, many children of God buy into his deceptions.

He is wicked. Another word for *wicked* is twisted, and he specializes in twisting the Word of God. He is quite capable of whispering into the soul of a religious person, "Kill them and I will raise them up." That sounds faintly like a word from the Bible.

When a thought such as that is taken in and meditated on by a person who has not been taught the difference between the voice of God coming from their born-again spirit and the voice of satan which can come through an unrenewed soul, a stronghold is established. Then satan can over a period of time, convince them to do the most terrible deeds. A stronghold is a house built by thoughts supplied by satan. Thank God, most of us never go as far with a deception as this young mother, or Jim Jones, or any number of other people who began right and ended up so wrong.

At the same time we must seek, as the Body of Christ, to protect our minds from deception. The soil that deception grows in must be washed by the Word until it is free from toxins, until it is able to bring forth fruits of righteousness—right living and right thinking.

The soil for our future is in the hidden ground of our souls (our mind, will, and emotions), and we must replace the negative core beliefs with positive core beliefs. This change can only come from the Word as we read, meditate, talk, and live out *who* we really are in God's eyes. As we *practice His presence* day after day, allowing Him to heal our past and paint beautiful new dreams for our future, only then will we be safe from wicked satanic seeds of destruction.

The Flipchart

We have by this time realized that the only way satan can get into our lives is through our mind, will, or emotions. The Holy Spirit of God lives in our born-again spirits, and where He lives satan cannot go. He has to go to where the Spirit and the Word are not resident. Unfortunately, few of us have been taught to actively pursue the renewing of our minds and reprogramming our souls until every word, voice, or leading is filtered through a rock-solid base of *Truth*.

In the wilderness, satan came to Jesus and tried his age-old trick of deception and half-truths using the Word. "*Go ahead, throw*

Yourself off the cliff. You know angels will keep You from getting hurt. You must be hungry...turn these stones into bread. If You will worship me, I will give to You the kingdoms of the world" (see Matthew 4:3-9). Jesus had a consistent answer for every one of satan's lies, twisting of the Word, and deceptions. He said, *"It is written...it is written...it is written"* (see Matthew 4:4-10).

Our problem has been that when the enemy of our souls comes to us and whispers lies, we don't know if it is written, what is written, or in what context it might have been written. We are likely to say, "Well that sounds spiritual to me..." and proceed to throw ourselves off the cliff. Battered and broken, we then get mad at God because the angels didn't show up.

Satan didn't make us jump, and he didn't push us. He just offered a suggestion. And because our souls were full of need, misinformation, unresolved issues and agendas, we added to his lies until a stronghold was erected and from the top of that edifice, we jumped—because it "seemed like the thing to do at the time," and it would fulfill a need in our wounded souls.

The enemy has a special flipchart he uses on Christian women, and depending on the state of our souls, we may reject one and accept another. A Christian woman may feel the urge to pray for her family and others who are hurting and in trouble. All at once, the thought of, "You don't even know how to pray," comes out of nowhere. But because she has just read a book about praying the Word, she rejects that one. Next the thought comes, "You aren't even saved." But he came too late on that one. She *knows* she is saved, and tells him so.

Then satan flips the chart, "Okay, you're saved, but remember all the ugly, ungodly things you did before that? Remember how you _____ (fill in the blank); therefore, you're lucky to even get in. Don't bother God with all those prayers. All have sinned and come short of the glory and you come up shorter than most. You're not worthy to pray for other people. You're low... just give it up."

And because all the things satan says are true, and she knows no Word about *who* she is in Christ Jesus, because no one has told her that the very Spirit of God is in her and because she has not visited the very heart of God by *practicing His presence,* she meekly agrees with the thought, resigning herself to worm status. She believes a lie, is deceived, and lives her entire Christian life in the dust and ashes of "what might have been."

If that isn't sad enough, her *assignment,* her *call,* her *passion* as an inspired intercessor, destined to shake the gates of hell, is lost to the Church and the world. And it started with one little thought, taken and processed through an unrenewed area of her mind with negative core values. Just one little thought.

To another woman of God he might whisper, "Drive off that bridge and then he will be sorry...."

If she reacts with, "No! That is a stupid thought," *flip* goes the chart. But a few days later after another fight with her husband he whispers, "Brother So-and-So is so sweet and kind. He smiled at you on Sunday." Because of unfulfilled needs in her soul, the attention of Brother So-and-So seems validating. She begins to think about Brother So-and-So...how he walks...how he shakes her hand...how he says nice things. The thoughts seem harmless enough, and they help her deal with the reality of a husband who has time and nice words for everybody but her.

Continuing to weave fantasies in her thought life, she thinks, *I wonder if Brother So-and-So would like this white dress on me.* The deception builds until she catches the eye of Brother So-and-So about the same time satan whispers in his ear, "That sure is a lovely woman." Because he too is lonely and has a collection of unmet needs and unresolved issues in his own soul. He is flattered and intrigued when she smiles at him.

After a while, satan goes off to plant other destructive thoughts into other wounded souls, leaving her and Brother So-and-So to take over his job. They continue meditating on the possibilities until a stronghold of deception is in place, bringing untold pain into two families and a church who looked up to them both. Unthinkable devastation. And it all began with one thought. One little thought processed by unrenewed souls void of the Word of God. One single thought. Who knew?

Circle of the Living Dead

Moving in the circle of the living dead
People who are alive, but just barely,
Never reaching out beyond
Their closely wrapped grave clothes
To touch the unseen…ask the unknown…
Or walk the far and distant paths of dreams.
God called us to Life and we take
That very Life and walk in it as men dead.
We are Christians…go to church…pay our dues
But the newborn capacity for wonder is gone.
We fear to ask our Maker, "Why am I here?"
"For what cause was I created?"
"What dreams can we dream together?"
Underneath our smoothed-over layer of contentment
Is the ever erupting question of "Isn't there more?"
Christ's answer shakes our world with reality—
"You can touch the unseen…know the unknown…
And walk the far and distant path of dreams.
Or…continue to move in the circle of the living dead
And die before you are fully born."

Assignments

THE KINGDOM OF DECEPTION

1. **Spend some quality time this week just sitting in His presence** and praying for the Body of Christ, as well as you, your family, and church.

2. **Put a guard over your soul** by writing word prayers in your journal from the Psalms and other Scripture. Sincerely pray and meditate on them until they begin to flow over onto your *morning pages.* That is when we know that our mind has been renewed to these truths. Remember we must have a rock-solid base of the Word of God to insure that we will not be deceived.

Such as:

I will serve God with all my heart and soul (Joshua 22:5, *Up Close and Personal*).

I know in all my heart and all my soul that not one thing has failed of all the good things that Father has promised me. All will come to pass for me, not one thing will fail (Joshua 23:14, *Up Close and Personal*).

For God alone my **soul** *waits in silence; from Him comes my total salvation [for my spirit, soul and body]. He is my rock and my salvation: my defense and my fortress. I shall not be greatly moved* (Psalm 62:1-2, *Up Close and Personal*).

In this Psalm we are talking to our soul, which is an excellent idea:

Soul, wait only upon God, silently submit to Him; for my hope and my expectation are in Him (Psalm 62:5, *Up Close and Personal*).

3. **Be sure to write your** *morning pages* every morning in order to gauge what your soul is up to. Considering all the things we have been learning about the enemy's tactics, we must be alert.

4. **How did the information gathered in the kingdom of deception affect you?**

Write it in your journal. Discuss it with a friend or study group. Tell Father.

Jesus said in John 14:30, "*The prince of this world comes but he finds no place in Me*" (*Up Close and Personal*). When the evil prince comes to you (and he will), will he find a place?

He won't...*if* our mind has been renewed by the Word of God...*if* the past wounds of our souls have been healed by the sacrifice of Jesus...*if* we are *practicing the presence* of our Father consistently...*if* our spirits are in charge and our souls are in position to hear the Holy Spirit's directions. Then, when he comes, he will find "no place" to deceive us.

Postscript Two—Strongholds in the Mind

We must defend our mind against thoughts of deception. A thought from satan, entertained and added to long enough, becomes a stronghold. When it becomes a stronghold, manifested evil follows. A stronghold blinds our minds so that light can't shine in. When we are in that condition, it is worse than useless for someone to argue with us. The more people try to straighten out our thinking, the more we argue. The more we restate our error, the more firmly we are stuck in that error. Only spiritual weapons can break down a stronghold. This arsenal is the Word of God.

In Second Corinthians 10:4-5, the Word tells us exactly what do with thoughts and how to even tear down the strongholds that may already be in place.

For the weapons of our warfare are not physical [weapons of flesh and blood], but they are mighty before God for the overthrow and destruction of strongholds. [Inasmuch as we] refute arguments and theories and reasonings and every proud and lofty thing that sets itself up against the [true] knowledge of God; and we lead every thought and purpose away captive into the obedience of Christ...(2 Corinthians 10:4-5, emphasis added).

Thoughts come to our mind, which is a function of our soul. When a thought comes that tries to go above the Word, we are to capture it. How? That's easy...by words. To be precise, by speaking out loud the Word of God. You cannot continue to think a thought and talk out loud at the same time. It cannot be done. Try it.

The Word of God spoken out loud takes captive whatever we are thinking. If a thought comes and says, "You are going to die," don't just sit there and meditate on that thought. Say, "No! I will live and not die! I rebuke that thought." You have just lead a thought, a satanic purpose, away captive that was trying to exalt itself against the Word of God. While you were speaking the Word, your soul had to shut up to see what your spirit had to say.

You have to stop the thoughts. Don't just sit there and THINK. The longer you think about a negative thought, the more negative thoughts will come. After a while you will develop a pattern of thinking, and before you know it, you will have a stronghold in your mind against the Word of God. That's when we begin to walk in deception.

Other translations say, "Cast down every thought..." or "Pull it down...." Protect your mind. Just say NO. Now that you know what to do when a negative thought comes, just do it.

The Kingdom of Excuses

WHAT COLOR IS YOUR PARACHUTE?

In the *Kingdom of Excuses* they make parachutes...very functional, multicolored parachutes. Christian women are not the only professional parachutists, but there are enough of us that we could start a club. We use them to bail out on ourselves. We use them to self-sabotage the *golden dream in the heart of God* for our lives. I have a friend who has lived in this *kingdom* for 20 years or more. I believe she runs one of the parachute factories. She is a pro at bailing out on herself. Maybe you know my friend. Maybe she lives at your house. She used to live at mine.

My friend is beautiful, articulate, educated, gifted, and called; but she cannot get from Point A to Point B in her life because she is forever analyzing Point A, or denying there is a Point B, or blaming Point A for stopping her progress to Point B. (I know it's confusing.)

As a classic codependent, she has also spent her entire life enabling everybody around her from progressing to Point B in their own lives and subsequently lost the God-given *assignment* she was born to accomplish. As an enabler to the wounded to stay wounded, she has a whole emotional encyclopedia of reasons why she and everybody around her have stopped at Point A...or even slipped back to Point O, setting up housekeeping, and furnishing grandly their household of pain and failure...in the *Kingdom of Excuses*.

My heart aches for my friend. By enabling, covering up for, and trying to fix everybody around her, she has lost herself. One moment she is full of lovely plans to move out into her gifts and *calling*; the next moment she needs prayer because she doesn't know what to do. Her beauty, her peace, her life, and her prophetic assignment have slipped unnoticed, uncelebrated, and unattained into a sea of pain...hers and others. She has lost her future trying to fix everybody's present. And the world has lost the gift she is.

Stop the Madness

We may be flying along at a high altitude leaving a jet stream behind us on our way to our *promised land*, and right before we land, we click into our "parachute mode" and bail out on ourselves. Our varied, colored parachutes are stored in our negative core beliefs, which we know are programmed into us and motivated by fear.

Funny thing (actually it's not so funny), the parachute we use most often as Christian women is the one of "religion." And when we strap it on our backs, we are fully convinced that we are "doing the right thing." Doing good for all the wrong reasons. We become well versed in suffering. We bear the cross. "Just leave me alone and let me enjoy my miserable moment." Some of us have created an art form with our years of self-doubt and insecurity.

For instance...you are a writer and have had a number of works published. People love your style—you can make them laugh and you can make them cry. At the same time you can make them think and want to know God better. Between writing articles, poetry, and a weekly newspaper column, you work on a book for two years. It's a good book and is accepted by a major Christian publishing house. The editor calls...she loves it...but it needs some tightening up...shortened a tad bit. So you tighten it up and send it back..."It's wonderful! But there is something missing in Chapter Three. In the rewrite it lost something." About this time in your life you are losing something too...your marriage.

Because the book is about you and your family, you put on a "religious-colored parachute" and tell yourself that you can't publish a book about a Christian family when you can't even keep a family together. Writing for Christian publications is something for others. Obviously you don't know what you're doing. If you did, this awful thing wouldn't be happening to you. So you stop taking calls from a confused editor, put the book on the shelf, and stop writing for publication for 20 years.

I wore that particular parachute and did a royal bailout on a God-given talent.

Parachutes are used in many different scenarios with the same pitiful results—a life of missed purpose and unfulfilled dreams. A codependent, verbally and/or physically abused woman can spend 25 years of her life covering up and trying to fix a relationship and a man whose basic core values are so "whacked" that he justifies clearly ungodly acts.

She lives her days and raises her children to tip-toe around their father, making excuses for a volatile manic depressant. They never know if he is going to explode in anger or cry in remorse for the way he acts.

Between "It's your fault I am like this..." and the heart-wrenching tears, it is usually the tears that make her strap on her parachute. He cries and she cries with him...because she loves him...because he has such potential...because maybe this time their "new beginning" will work.

She puts on her parachute when he brings her a cup of coffee before she gets out of bed in the morning...or picks her a rose from their garden. Never mind that her heart and sometimes her body is black and blue from the day before. Sometimes she will cry for hours and hours from loneliness, "God help me...God help me." Then she will dry her tears and go fix him a nice dinner. Maybe tonight, if everything is perfect, he will look at her and smile. Crumbs from the king's table.

All this time they are active in church and well-thought-of in the community. All this time she dutifully has her quiet time, reads the Word, and prays. All this time she is strapped into her parachute and living a lie.

Then one day, by the grace of God and no doubt resulting from the consistent reprogramming brought about by the daily Word going into her soul, she wakes from her self-induced coma and says, "I need help."

By some divine intervention from her Father, she has recently met a pastor who is known for his "no-nonsense, cut-to-the-chase, what-is-your-problem" style of ministry. So our parachute lady opens up and tells the whole sordid story, leaving out no detail. That is a major breakthrough in itself. And when she is finished, she breathes a sigh of relief. At least someone else on earth knows the hell she has lived in for 25 years.

The pastor stays quiet through the whole replay of the insanity. When parachute lady finally winds down, pastor hands her a Kleenex™ and says, "Why on earth have you stayed?" It is then that she begins to spread out the many parachute excuses that she has used to keep herself out of the will of God for her life. All of them are the color of "religion."

"Well, *I* thought that if *I* could 'First Corinthians 13 (the love chapter) it' long enough, he would change.

"*I* thought if *I* could give enough, pray enough, be submissive enough...he would change.

"*I* thought *I* had to keep the family together.

"*I* thought *I* was his anchor to reality."

After listening to the repetitive "I thought I" monolog for several minutes, pastor looks her straight in the eye and says, "Move over, Jesus; we got a new Savior."

With those eight little words her religious parachute is shredded into uselessness. Reality has once again taken on religion, and won. Speechless (for a change), she sits there mentally fingering the torn fragments of her carefully crafted parachute and faces the truth.

She can't save anybody.

Jesus has already done that.

She can't suffer enough to make him whole.

Jesus has already done that.

She isn't called by God to be crucified for another's sins.

Jesus had already done that.

He is the Savior...she is not.

When she looks up into pastor's eyes, she knows and pastor knows that the *kingdom of excuses* is history. As she stands to leave, the pastor says, "Hold out your hands." When she does, they are in their customary clinched position. "Now open them up and empty them.

The Lord is saying to you, 'You have held the past so tightly clenched in your hands that I couldn't get you to take all the wonderful gifts that belong to you. Now, open your hands, empty them, turn loose, make room for the gift of a new life.' "

And so she does. The shredded religious colored parachute she leaves in a heap on the floor. She won't need it now. She is going to learn to fly and not even take a parachute with her. No more excuses. She has heard the *Truth* and the *Truth* has set her free.

Another professional parachutist said to me just last week,

"I stayed over 20 years...20 years of being beaten, shoved, spit on, called every vile name in the book. One time he hit me so hard I lost our baby. Seven years ago, I went to a battered woman's shelter with my children...but he cried and the reasoning (excuses) began...

"But he is my children's father.

"He has the income...how can I support my children?

"I don't want to raise my kids on welfare.

"I am a Christian and divorce is wrong.

(Parachutes. Parachutes. Parachutes.)

"Strangely, every time I came up with an excuse, I would hear this still small voice inside:

"I am your Father.

"I am your support...not man.

"I look out for your welfare.

"He broke the covenant...you didn't.

"But he cried and I went back. All this time I was going to church, talking to God, and reading the Word. I got to the place where I could hear the voice of God speaking to me in my spirit. One day He said to me, 'If you go, I am going to be with you; if you stay, I am going to be with you; the decision is yours. If you empty your hands, I will fill them.' "

The night she fled for the last time, she grabbed her children and climbed out a window as he was trying to break in the door they had barricaded. She finally knew deep in her heart that Father didn't create her to live like this. He has more for her and her girls. As she told me this story, the clarity in her beautiful blue eyes said more than she could put into words. She is going after her *reality*. She is going to be who Father created her to be. She is going to step out on *faith* and expect the net to be there. She is going to go for it. All we can say is, "You go, Girl!"

What If?

When I have asked women who have emerged for "the last time," how their lives would have been different if they had left fifteen, ten, five, or even two years earlier, this is what I hear:

"I would have escaped a lot of tears, pain, and regret."

"My children would not have been so hurt."

"My children would not be so much like their role-model dad."

"I would have been free to dream."

"I would have had a life—a car, a job, a home—by now."

So all your parachute excuses were wrong?

"Yes, they were; and yes, they are."

One thing about parachutes—they don't stop the fall; they just prolong the trip.

So What's Up With That?

Traveling toward *Peace*
Means traveling to Wholeness;
It means being *Centered*
Not reactive...just responsive.

Doing well and almost there
Something strange happens;
I find I am running backward
Stymied...perplexed...confused.

What's up with this?
I am not that person.
Where did she come from?
The past is present again.

Assignments

THE KINGDOM OF EXCUSES

1. **When you hear, "Jump and the net will appear,"** what is your first reaction? Be honest. Maybe your response is, "Easy for you to say." Actually, it's not easy for me to say...I've done it. Free falling is not easier than parachuting. But I can say, the net was there.

2. **So what color is your parachute?** Are you living your best life? If not, why not? Write the answers in your journal.

3. **About your morning pages...are you doing them every morning?** If not, why not? Do they seem useless to you? Silly? Could that be your soul giving its opinion? If so, I wonder what it is trying to hide? Don't bail out on *your morning pages.*

   Do the morning pages first thing every morning—three pages of whatever. Just show up and do them. Remember: Don't read them until this journey is completed. We want to empty our soul, not meditate upon its "stuff."

   DO NOT SHARE YOUR MORNING PAGES...WHAT IS THERE IS STRICTLY BETWEEN YOU AND FATHER!

   Travel Note: *Morning pages* can at times turn into *practicing the presence.* If something is bothering you, go to the pages and ask Father. I did that when I was trying to clarify the connection between spirit, soul, and body for this book. I

155

knew how it worked, but being a lover of clarity, I needed a way to write it so that others could understand. This is exactly what happened:

Me: "Father, help me make this very plain." (I wait pen in hand, then I start writing.)

Father: "Tell them it is exactly like the chain of command in the war." And the illustration you read about in Chapter Four flowed onto the *morning pages*.

4. **Are you finding yourself *practicing His presence* at odd times...not *only* in the designated time slot?** Like, when you're cooking dinner, watching TV, vacuuming, etc.? That's a good thing. *He really is there, you know.*

5. **Are you adding minutes every week to your time with Father?** If you have added five minutes a week since we began this journey nine weeks ago, you ought to be spending 50 minutes each day this week **practicing His presence**. Part of that time could be spent reading *His love letters* to you, His Word, *Up Close and Personal*.

    Such as:

    My precious daughter, I will not in any way fail you...nor give you up...nor leave you without support. I will not, I will not, I will not in any degree leave you helpless...nor forsake you...nor let you down or relax My hold on you...assuredly not! So take comfort and be encouraged and confidently and boldly say, "My Father is my helper; I will not be seized with alarm. I will not fear...or dread...or be terrified. What can mere man do to me? (Hebrews 13:5b-6, paraphrased from the Amplified Bible, *Up Close and Personal*).

    Read the Word aloud. Create with your mouth what you are reading with your eyes.

A Postscript

God is not going to do anything about our miserable circumstances.

Jesus did it all (past tense).

Our part is in trusting that if I step out on His Word, even if I can't see it, the net will be there.

The Kingdom of the Unresolved

A Strange Land

In the *Kingdom of the Unresolved*, things can get pretty weird. You're traveling at a good rate of speed, making excellent time, and all of a sudden, it is as if you are hallucinating. You know you are not the same woman who began this trip, and yet you hit a bump in the road and WHAM…you are whacked up side of the head with a reaction straight out of your long forgotten past.

Somebody or something just hit a button.

Button…Button…Who's Got the Button?

As we journey through this *kingdom*, we will talk about a variety of buttons. Some buttons turn things off and on; some buttons save things; and as I recently discovered, some buttons can delete three days of work on a manuscript. Then there is my favorite—the buttons we find on clothes.

Over the years of working with old fabric and other textiles in my *Out of the Attic* business of making dolls, I have developed a fondness for buttons. Actually it is more like a fixation. I love buttons—large fancy ones, tiny antique pearl ones—really just any button. For years it seemed that buttons were trying to "talk" to me. I didn't understand it, and sometimes I thought I was losing it. Talking buttons was a little "out there." I must admit I felt better after reading a book about George Washington Carver called *The Man Who Talked to Flowers*. The book said that Mr. Carver talked to flowers and asked them to give up their secrets…and they talked back to him.

I have yet to hear a button speak, but one thing I do know is when something arrests my attention, the Holy Spirit is trying to get a truth across to me—an object lesson or a parable—and I have a "God-is-in-the-details moment."

In our Women of Peace Ministry Center located in El Paso, Texas, we have a unique gift shop called *Peace*, full of one-of-a-kind creations designed mainly from things people throw away. The whole place is an *Out of the Attic* experience. Every item there "speaks" to the women who come through our doors. They speak of *new beginnings*. They speak that even throwaways can become art in the right hands. They speak of how Father looks at His daughters.

Needless to say, you can't look around in *Peace* very long before you notice the buttons. Not only are they on the dolls, but you will discover them on cards, refrigerator magnets, bookmarks, wall hangings, and anything else that will stand still long enough to get a button glued on. However, when we first began creating things for the shop, I still didn't really know what they were trying to say to me.

Then one day, as a lady was looking around while I was on duty in that part of the Ministry Center, she said, "You have buttons on everything...is there a reason?" Without stopping to think, the answer rose up out of my spirit and surprised even me. "Buttons," I said with confidence, "stand for closure. The Women of God need to have closure on some of the things in their past so they can walk into their future. Buttons are a reminder." The lady answered, "That makes sense." And I thought, *Yes it does. Wow, Father, that really does make sense. Thanks.*

A long, long time ago as a child in the Appalachian Mountains, I remember playing a game with my mom and brother called "Button, button, who's got the button?" The leader would have a button and pretend to deposit it into each person's hand. Of course, only one person would have the button or perhaps the leader would keep it. In retrospect, I can't figure out why that was so much fun...but it was. Chalk it up to a kid's ability to find delight in the little things.

One night at a *Women of Peace* meeting, we talked about the buttons of unresolved issues in our soul that satan can push. The difference between my childhood game and the one satan plays is, the owner of the button doesn't know she has the button until it is pushed and activates a reaction that has zero to do with reality. Unresolved issues are usually buried so deep and covered so cleverly that we think they have gone away...until satan pushes a button.

This is how it happens. We are progressing in our Christian life. We are renewing our mind with the Word of God. We are spending time alone every day *practicing His presence*. We have dutifully copied into our *journal* the Word, putting our name in it thereby making it *Up Close and Personal*. We are rocking along pretty well, enjoying more *peace* than ever before in our lives. We're learning. We begin to think, *Wow, I am finally free from the bondages of my past*. We may even be entertaining the thought, *So this is what wholeness feels like*. Then satan shows up to play the button game.

Because we are doing all the right things, because we at last know who our enemy is, and because we are making progress, satan simply cannot drop any new deception into our souls. His days of stealing, killing, and destroying are over in our lives. We are wise to him. We are not going to take one of his lies and meditate on it until we bring it to pass. We have too much Word in us; we are too acquainted with the *presence of God*; and we have come too far to go back now.

Since he can find no new place to attack us, he goes looking through the archives of our past to see if there are any unhealed hurts or painful core beliefs from previous wounds. He searches to see if we really and truly have exposed all our soulish issues to the healing power in the *grace of God*, or if we have buried it so deep we do not know it is still there.

We almost never see it coming, but all of a sudden someone will say something and trigger a reaction that has little to do with what they are talking about. Past all reasoning, past all truth deposited into our souls, past all real growth we have experienced, comes the pain, hurt, fear, and rejection that you would have sworn to be in the past— satan has just pushed a button.

One such incident stands out clearly in my mind. It stands out clearly because it happened only a few weeks ago. Beginning early on, as a child of a young single mother in the Appalachian Mountains, I learned money was never to be spent on useless items. The definition of "useless items" was anything that didn't fill a basic need of food, shelter, and clothes. I'm talking *basic* here—no frills, nothing fancy, the most basic of basics.

The fear of spending a dollar uselessly was reenforced and built upon in almost every close relationship in my life. I had developed a basic core belief that it was thoughtless, selfish, and almost always made somebody mad if I spent money on myself uselessly. Even when I did spend, I invariably went to the sale rack and ended up buying something that was "okay" but not "me." The color was wrong or the fit not quite right. Most of the time I just hung it in my closet and rarely wore it because it didn't make me feel special. When I did wear it and someone made a comment about it, I would feel the need to justify or *excuse* my purchase, explaining that it was on sale.

This stronghold on my soul continued even after I had all the money I needed to buy whatever I wanted. After I moved out of a "poverty mentality," I got stuck in a "sale rack" mentality. As I progressed along to healing and wholeness, God gave me the strength to act on truth, and supernaturally moved me out of my life situations that had controlled me with this fear. I was no longer a victim. I was free.

Not only was I delivered from controlling spirits that had kept me in bondage, but by His grace and mercy, Father placed into my life a wonderful, generous, prosperous man who treats me like a queen. My husband of two years, at this writing, is all a woman could ever want. He loves, validates, and encourages me to be free to pursue my dreams.

Like I said, I had come such a long way. I thought that mind-set, that negative core belief, or stronghold of my past was just that…past. Months and months had come and gone with absolutely no sign that I wasn't totally free, when this old fear came barreling out of my soul, full-fleshed and paralyzing as ever.

I can't remember exactly what my husband said; it was possibly about some bills we needed to pay—just a simple everyday comment said in passing. Then he went to work and I went shopping. I had just picked up a dollar item (one dollar, mind you!), which I didn't really need but wanted, when WHAM! out of my soul came all the confusion, uncertainty, and fear that I had so carefully hidden underneath all the wholeness God was building into my mind, will, and emotions.

I was stunned. What on earth was this all about? I stood there with more than enough money to buy whatever I wanted and the hand holding a dollar item was trembling, indecision and bewilderment engulfing me. Like a VCR replaying a bad horror movie, somewhere from deep in my soul, fear sprang up and in 3-D technicolor. All the familiar symptoms—the knot in the pit of my stomach, the frantic search for an excuse in case I got caught—it was all there. Fear from a hidden wound in my soul, and I had no idea it was there.

Talk about being confused. Here I was, actively in the ministry of helping women get free from their soulish issues so they can embrace their future. For years and years, week after week, class after class, on television and in our church, I taught about the beauty of a soul set free. And here I was, behind the bars of a prison I didn't even know existed in me. The enemy of my soul, satan, had just pushed a button.

Thank God, I had enough wholeness active in my soul and was well versed in *practicing the presence* that I stopped immediately and began to deal with this flashback of fear. I almost always use pen and paper to talk to Father. (It helps me keep track of our conversations.) So as the reality of what was happening in me hit my spirit, I grabbed my notepad out of my purse, and we began to have a heart-to-heart. I have learned to handle satan head-on…don't stay in bondage a single minute longer than necessary. When we are dealing with an attack on our eternal soul, it pays not to waste time. Truth sets us free. The Truth of what Father knew about this attack was in my spirit where He lives, and so I *centered* in to get His perspective of the situation.

Standing in the aisle of a busy department store oblivious to the people around me, I wrote:

Father, what is this in me? What's the deal about how I feel about money? At this very moment, I feel like I am right back in the grips of a controlling spirit and have to account for every penny I spend. Where did this come from? Where do I stand inside of me? What is in me that can be so full of fear that I am right back in a victim mode?

Then the wholeness in me sprang up:

Father, I am not going to live this way! This is not part of who I am! Father, you do whatever it takes inside of me to get me free from this thing. Heal me, make me whole, deliver me. My days of living with this hidden wound are over. Not one more minute, no more, not now, not ever! Period. Thank you for showing me the Truth. From this day forward, I am free.

On that day, I saw the plan of the enemy for what it was—an attack using the unresolved issues in my soul. I saw how he had gained entrance into my mind and emotions. That day satan overplayed his hand. That day the "button," that inroad into my soul was lost to him forever. That day the "button game" was over in that area of my life. That day I won, and took one more giant step into my *promised land*...into my personal *Peaceful Kingdom.*

When I shared this story at our Women of Peace meeting, one of the gals asked, "Well, did you buy the dollar item?" "Oh, Girlfriend," I replied, "I filled my cart!"

What's Up With That?

As we continue to replace the negative core beliefs with positive core beliefs from the Word of God, we also need to constantly monitor what is happening in us. We must look objectively at the reaction that comes out of us and other people. The way we react when something happens is a real, no-fail barometer of what is in our souls. Sometimes we will have a "sleeper" that lies silent for a while; then from out of nowhere it will blast us with an assignment from hell. Keep constantly in mind that our goal is to have our souls and bodies subjected to our spirits where Father, Son, and Holy Spirit lives, dwells, and makes their home.

As we are learning, we can fool ourselves in how well we are doing. Bottom line—*if we have a **problem** with anybody or anything, **we** have a problem.* Oh, they may indeed have a problem, but the real problem for us is how we react to their problem. A soul set free never reacts...only responds.

This whole subject reminds me of a story I read somewhere. This guy heard the doorbell ring, and when he went to answer it, the only thing he found was a snail sitting on the porch. He picked up the snail, hauled off and threw it as far as he could, and went back inside slamming the door behind him. Three years later, he heard the doorbell again and opened the door to find the same snail sitting there. The snail said to him, "So, what was *that* all about?" I guess the moral of the story is no matter how long it takes to get to the bottom of a reaction, get there and find out what "*that*" is all about.

Here are a few examples of "buttons" and possible reactions, depending on our negative or positive core beliefs, learned responses, and personality types. All show the condition of our souls at any given moment.

Scenario One Reaction

Someone, like a boss or a family member, says or does something that makes us mad or hurts our feelings. If we are a passive-aggressive victim type, we won't say a word to that person, but when we get home, our family and friends will hear about it for hours, and even days and weeks. We have a great capacity to suffer grandly and at length.

Or, if we internalize it, we will find that hurt coming out of nowhere (we think), at another time and another place. For instance, our husband may say something to us in a tone of voice that is reminiscent of how someone in our past used to talk to us. And all the anger, pain, the "I'm-not-taking-anymore-of-this" attitude comes roaring out of "somewhere," and we unleash a torrent of reaction totally out of proportion to the comment made by our hapless husband. The "somewhere" all that came out of is the part of our souls that is full of everything except the Word of God.

Internalized wounds can also manifest themselves in physical sickness. If we have a chronic illness that is not responding to medicine and prayer, or keeps recurring, it is a really wise decision to search our soul for unresolved issues. I can't tell you of the times over the years that someone has asked me to pray for them, and the Holy Spirit has moved me to ask if they have unforgiveness or hidden anger. When they are able to acknowledge and forgive, their healing is manifested quickly. When our souls and our bodies learn to take direction from our spirit man, full of the wisdom of God, they will work in the perfection for which they were designed.

Scenario Two Reaction

Somebody close to us tears into us saying things that would have torn our hearts out as a passive-aggressive victim. But the moment they start, we recognize that they are moving out of their own wounded past, and all that anger has more to do with them than it has to do with us.

Instead of hurt, all we feel is empathy. We remember when we acted or felt the same way, desperately trying to find peace and order in our lives by blaming somebody else for a problem. We remember the driving urge to "straighten somebody else out" when all the time it was us who was in turmoil. We remember how we felt "led" to "have a talk" with someone so they could see the error of "their" ways...when all the time the "leading" was coming out of our own wounded soul.

We have been meditating on who we are in Christ Jesus. We have reprogrammed our soul by reading the Word and have spent quality time, *pacticing His presence.* We are learning that we do not have to justify or defend ourselves anymore. We no longer live by another's light or what they think about us; we live by our own *Inner Light.* So when they let go with a string of "This-is-what-I-think-your-problem-is" tirade, we find ourselves, to our utter amazement saying, in a gentle controlled voice, "That was uncalled for, unkind, and unacceptable. You may not talk to me that way."

When this happens the first few times, we are as shocked as the other person is. Where did *that* come from? It came out of a soul set free. A victimized soul could not have answered like that...a free soul could. When this scenario happened to me for the first time, I was amazed to hear those very words come out of my mouth, when in the past, Scenario One would have been my reaction.

A person with a soul set free has a unique ability to calmly step outside of themselves and their situations. They can observe objectively what is going on in their lives and in the lives of the people around them. In a soul set free, there is no fear; therefore, it has no need to defend itself. In a soul set free, there are no "buttons" for satan to push.

Mirror Check

When I share this concept at *Women of Peace* meetings, I challenge the ladies to practice stepping outside every situation that is pushing the buttons of their souls. Every time anger, rejection, impatience, hurt, or resentment rises up, or comes out of their mouth, they are to stop, go look in a mirror, and ask themselves, *"Just what part of your born-again spirit, led by the Holy Spirit, did that come out of?"*

Answer: No part. It came out of a wounded soul. Not the "real us" dominated by the Holy Spirit. He has no unresolved issues, impatience, sin, or problems with rejection. He never tries to defend Himself against a damaged soul's opinion. He doesn't have to. He knows the end from the beginning. He knows the *plan.* He has no negative emotions in Him. All He has in Him is *love, joy, peace, patience, kindness, goodness, faithfulness, gentleness, and self-control.* (See Galatians 5:22-23.) It's called "the fruit of the Spirit." And when our souls are healed and filled with the concepts of God, and we are in position to hear Him, we too will be known for our *love, joy, peace, patience, kindness, goodness, faithfulness, gentleness, and self-control.*

That is what was in Jesus' soul when He walked the earth; and when satan came to Him, he could find no place. The time is quickly approaching that when satan even dares to try playing one of his "button games" in our mind, will, or emotions, his failure is assured, because in *us,* he will find no place.

Casual Death

Nature is full of casual death—
Leaves…grass…trees
Sprout…unfurl…and die,
Returning to their source.
There is no battle,
No resistance, only submission
To the higher plan.

My life too should be
Full of casual death,
Dying to the self
That nurtures pain and fear.
Even my will
And with that death
New life begins.

As with nature…so with me.

Assignments

The Kingdom of the Unresolved

This is the week to ask, "What's up with that?" Cut yourself no slack, no matter how long it takes get to the bottom of every negative reaction.

1. **Confronting the issues:** Possible reactions to double-check—what comes out of me when the following buttons are pushed? Record your answers in your *journal.*

   - *Traffic is impossible and I'm late.*

   - *The children just got on my last nerve.*

   - *My husband snapped my last nerve.*

   - *My mom, dad, husband, anybody…tries to lay a guilt trip on me.*

   - *My boss treats me unfairly. I didn't get the raise, promotion, etc.*

   - *A salesperson or waitperson doesn't know the meaning of customer service.*

   - *You waited six weeks for a special order and they sent the wrong size, color, style.*

   - *The preacher says something that goes against your preconceived, preprogrammed idea of "whatever."*

   - *You get put on hold for 30 minutes and then are disconnected.*

   - *You are believing God for the rent money and it's late.*

Concerning the latter... Father knows it is more important for us to realize what issues in our souls need attention
than for Him to supply demands on our time schedules.
Rent money is no problem to God. He does and will *"supply all our needs according to His riches in glory by Christ Jesus"*
(Philippians 4:19 KJV). Trust me...that is some kind of serious riches. There is no lack. Abundance is one of His names.
El Shaddai means "He is more than enough."

Father More Than Enough has a million ways to get your rent
money...but if there is a problem in our souls that is causing the lack, we will continue to run back up on the same
problem again and again.

Note about root causes: Better to get the root fixed than
specialize in trying to fix bad fruit. What is in us will manifest in our lives. This week we are inspecting fruit...and
pulling up roots.

2. **Note in your journal** any other "buttons" you detected.
   After confronting the "reaction," simply ask Father to heal
   in your soul whatever the basic problem is. He will.

3. **Is spending time** *practicing His presence* easier now? If you
   have added five minutes to each day during our *journey*,
   you will be spending 50 minutes *consciously* enjoying His
   company...on the *morning pages* as well as whenever He
   wants to talk.

   Wonderful side effect of spending *time in the presence:*
   We have a tendency to act and even look like *who* we hang
   around with. The folks in Jesus' day looked at the disciples
   and *"saw that they had been with Jesus"*(Acts 4:13).

4. **Do morning pages.** Continually remind yourself that these
   pages are just another form of meditation. They will locate
   exactly where your soul is daily. Yes, this exercise costs
   something (time and discipline), but you and your future
   are worth it. You have a *full-of-glory life* waiting for you. The
   whole *plan* is in your human spirit, and once your spirit is in
   charge, the *plan* will unfold.

The Kingdom of Death

THE END OF THE QUICK FIX

The *Kingdom of Death* is not as foreboding as it sounds. It is also known as *dying to self, embracing the larger plan, and the end of the quick fix*. In this *kingdom,* we lay down yet another area of our negative soul life as we embrace the larger plan for ourselves and for the people around us. This is rocky terrain, so we better get on our hiking boots, and for safety's sake, they better include some steel toes for protection. Because in this *kingdom,* there are some issues that can do serious damage by stepping on our toes.

Until Death Do Us Part

Yes, that is a line from the traditional wedding vows. Of course, it can apply to other areas as a metaphor, but for the time being we will take it for what it is—a reference to marriage. I know that not all of us are married or even want to be. Some of us have been there and done *that* too many times to ever want to go back. But if you are, were, want to be, or know somebody who is (how's that for a catchall), then this section will hold vital information, even if you only pass it on.

In all the years I have ministered to women, I have consistently run into a deception that married women are prone to entertain. That's when, "Til death us do part" takes on a life of its own. It happens when a woman's "unresolved issues" run head-on into her husband's negative core beliefs, and she begins to fantasize his "sooner-not-later departure."

169

It actually is not as drastic as a friend of mine stated years ago half in jest. She was relaying the ongoing saga of a Christian husband living and planning their lives out of a seriously wounded soul. This had gone on and on for so many years that I finally asked her if she had ever considered divorce. Her answer was a classic, "Divorce no…murder yes."

Few of us seriously consider murder, but many of us entertain the possibility, the prayer, mind-set, desire, and expectation that, "If God can't fix that man, then He ought to just take him off the earth, so I can get on with my life." Few women living out of a wounded past, married to a man with his own bundle of baggage, escape this fantasy, and will entertain this thought at least for a passing moment. The really hard-core escapists can find Scripture to backup what they think God ought to do about that impossible man.

This fantasy can expand into a number of directions: for instance, planning the funeral and burial plot (all in her mind of course), a need to buy more life insurance, figuring up how much social security she will draw when the primary breadwinner is no longer amongst us, stocking up on Kleenex for all the crying one must do at a funeral. Yes, I do have a vivid imagination, but I honestly did not "make up" one of these examples. All came straight from the sources of these, hopefully passing, fantasies.

Of course, this is not usually a 24/7 flight of imagination that goes on for years. It is a sporadic "quick fix" we pull out of our wounded souls when his wounded soul crosses us. Then the spiritual giant *we think* we are just *knows* "**God must do something!**" basically, "**Get him out of here.**"

One *Woman of Peace* who is a minister in her own right, laughed when I told her I was writing about this subject. She said I could use her as an illustration. She is married to a wonderful, charming, and gifted man of God. They serve their church in leadership positions today…but this was not always the case. Due to a fair amount of negative core beliefs, programmed into each of them from childhood, Jim and Susan had "opinions" that often differed. Despite a dedication and undeniable love for each other, their 20-plus years had been riddled with turmoil. Then they got saved and the "fun" really began.

As sometimes happens, Susan got saved first and began going to church, and Jim followed. That's all they knew to do. In the particular church where they landed, they had no teaching on how to renew the mind, or actually how-to anything that had to do with their souls. They heard a lot of how they were supposed to act, but no one really told them what must be done before they would even be able to live a victorious life. All they knew was they loved God so they went to church.

Because of imbedded insecurities and the wounds in his soul, Jim especially, never wanted to stay at a church very long. Someone always offended him. Either the pastor preached too much about tithing, or somebody didn't speak to him, or something happened. Naturally, satan saw that his "buttons" were periodically pushed. There was a little of that, "I'm-the-*man*-and-I-know" thing going on, and the little woman submitted. That's the way they lived out the first part of their Christian life—going from one church to another, searching for who knows what, not knowing that *the problem* of church-hopping was with them, namely their unrenewed mind, will, and emotions.

Then one night, Susan walked into a *Women of Peace* meeting, and something deep within her responded to the teaching. Her born-again spirit with its hungry soul had an "Aha moment." We didn't know that night that Father had just done a divine hookup.

There was a terrible rainstorm that evening, and in the hot dry climate of El Paso, Texas, that in itself is an event. Usually, when it rains torrents in the desert, people just stay home and look out the window. But that night, a dozen or more women from all parts of the city and even from New Mexico, found themselves sitting around a table in a church fellowship hall. Susan had been invited by a friend to come. The power had gone off all over the city, and by candlelight I shared some of the concepts in this book.

After the meeting, I didn't see Susan for over a year. But the Holy Spirit was at work and from time to time, she would remember that night when the rains came and she first heard "reality" by candlelight.

One Sunday morning, she walked into the same church where I attended, not knowing that I was also there. After the service, she reminded me of that stormy night across town. She said she had never forgotten the things she heard, and something had happened to her that evening.

Susan became a faithful part of the *Women of Peace*. She was there, taking notes every time the doors opened. At the *Women of Peace* meetings, we consistently and in-depth, deal with renewing the mind, confronting unresolved issues of the soul, and healing of past wounds. Because of her faithfulness, Susan began to experience some real spiritual growth.

One of the "last frontiers" of her soul that she needed to deal with was her impatience with Jim and his lack (in her estimation) of spiritual growth. "That man is impossible!" she would rage. "He won't pay tithes, he cusses, he's always wanting to change churches...." "He...he...he...!" She even kept a list of his trespasses and in her "righteous superiority" would relay them to God (as if He didn't know). "Did You see that, God? Did You hear what he said to me? God, You are going to have to do something! I'm not going to live this way. He's holding me back"...and on and on. The "grand finale" that she laid on God was, "If You can't fix him, take him." "Take him" loosely translated is "Kill him, God, and deliver me from my misery."

She became so fed up and tired of waiting on God to "take him" that she considered other measures. One day I asked her how they were doing, and she with great exasperation said, "Well, I guess I'm just going to have to divorce that man." I turned away to hide my grin. I had seen it too many times and I knew the symptoms.

Wholeness Cometh...

What experience and the Spirit of God had taught me was that wholeness was being built into Susan. As she read the Bible *Up Close and Personal*, wrote in her *journal*, prayed, *practiced the presence*, stayed faithful to her church, and continued to deal with her own soulish issues, that wholeness was coming. There would come a time when she would realize that Jim was not her problem. She was her problem, and if God "took him," she would still be stuck with herself. As long as the negative core beliefs were resident in her soul, it wouldn't matter if she had a perfect man (if such a creature existed); she would still be faced with the same issues.

Yes, no doubt Jim had some problems, as his reactions on certain subjects proved. There was possibly lots of room for improvement in her husband. But as we learned last week, a "whole woman" moves out of her *center*, led and guided by the Holy Spirit, not in the quick-fix tendencies of her soul. A whole woman, healed, delivered, and walking in the revelation of how a wounded soul can mess up a perfectly good person, can walk in *peace* no matter how others act. She simply does not buy into their issues; she stays *centered*, believing Father can and will "*perfect that which concerns her.*" A whole woman embraces the larger plan, and that includes wholeness for her loved ones too.

She has learned "strategic disengagement." In other words, she knows she cannot have toxic overconcern about other people's growing edges. She knows *she* is not the Holy Spirit and *she* can't change anybody. All that is Father's territory. The best thing she can do for her loved ones is to get, be, and stay whole herself.

Susan "got it." But before she "got it," she got a wake-up call straight from Father. She had been spending hours and hours praying, asking Father what she was supposed to do with her life. She wanted a "ministry." She wanted to take the love of God to the far corners of the globe. She wanted to share all she was learning with the lost and dying world. She wanted to preach, pray, and be a gift to everyone who knew her. One day after an extended time of bombarding Heaven with "When-do-I-get-my-ministry?" prayers, Father spoke, "How can I give you a ministry when you can't even love your husband?"

Needless to say, that question rocked her back on her prayer wheels. She had learned to hear His voice...and she had learned to obey. She had heard enough about the "cold water ministry" of the Holy Spirit that she immediately knew what this really meant. The *Up Close and Personal* interpretation was: "*If you ever want to fulfill your call, you better renew your mind in the area of how you treat your husband. You need to get this 'soul issue' taken care of and become the woman I created you to be. If you can live it at home, you can live it anywhere. If I can trust you to love Jim, I can trust you to love My other hurting children. I want purity from the inside out, in every area of your life...not just when you are on your knees.*" She "got it"...and their lives have never been the same.

Because of her diligence to renew her mind with the Word, her acceptance of Father's correction, and her humility to quickly repent and ask Jim's forgiveness, she laid a foundation for a worldwide ministry. Because of the *love, joy, peace, and wholeness* in her; *love, joy, peace, and wholeness* are coming to her whole family; and many people are coming to the knowledge of the truth.

Jim? Well, considering the twinkle in his eye the last time I saw him, the *peace* that radiates out of Susan's face, the way they hold hands in church, and the way *they* pray over *their* tithes, I'd say they were beginning to enjoy *days of Heaven on earth.* Like every woman who "gets it," Susan is giving birth to what is in her. That's how the system works.

A Wake-up Call

Another member of the "take him" club related how God jerked the slack out of her tendency to move toward this fantasy when she experienced a vivid dream. In her dream she was wearing a long-sleeve, white dress (which is a good start...as a symbol, a white dress could stand for a robe of righteousness). In her lovely white dress she was doing wonderful works. Then something happened (the husband-soul, flare-up thing); all her good works stopped and out from under the sleeve of her pure white robe of righteousness a dead bird fell. The bird had been dead for a long time, and it was covered with mites. When she raised her sleeve, she could see that the mites had eaten into the skin of her arm. The Holy Spirit told her that even though she was saved, white and pure, doing many good works, she had death up her sleeve. The death mites were eating into her covering (skin). The effect was a hampering of the beauty of her arm, or how she reached out to the world.

Did she consider this a wake-up call? Definitely. Question is... do we?

David's Soul Flare-Up

Surprisingly, women do not have a monopoly on the "take them" soul issue. The Word of God gives us a classic example on this theme and the "fantasizing pray-er" was none other than King David himself. In the incomparably beautiful Psalm 139, we get a glimpse of David's soul having a "death-up-its-sleeve moment." (Sometimes I wonder if some of David's Psalms came out of *his* version of *morning pages.* There sure is a mixture of negative and positive core beliefs represented.) For instance, the first 18 verses of this Psalm, David is waxing poetic about the wonders of God's intimate love for him. (Turn back to Week Four for an *Up Close and Personal* look at the first 18 verses of Psalm 139.)

After a wonderful time of inspiration, enlightenment, and revelation knowledge coming to David, check out verses 19 through 22: *"If You would only slay the wicked, O God...and make them depart from me. They speak against You...they take Your name in vain!"* [Next David gets a little pious.] *"Do I not hate them, O Lord, who hate You? Am I not grieved and do I not loathe them who rise up against You? Yes, I hate them with a perfect hatred! They have become my enemies"* (paraphrased from the Amplified Bible, *Up Close and Personal,* emphasis added). Sound familiar?

*But...*in verses 23 and 24, David gets right back where we must get when we begin to have these "death wishes": *"Search me [thoroughly], O God, and know my heart [soul]! Try me and know my thoughts! And see if there is any wicked or hurtful way in me, and lead me in the way everlasting"* (emphasis added). David went right back into the presence and got help for his wayward soul. That is the only place to take such off-the-wall fantasy.

We as women of the *endtime glorious Church* must give our mates and the people we live with the same room to grow that Father has given us. We absolutely have to grow up into who we really are—*royal daughters of the Most High God.* We need to get over ourselves, and stop trying to make the people around us act like *we* think they should act. We must get it into our souls that *they* can't make us happy no matter what they do. Only Father holds the key to our happiness, and He has placed that happiness, fulfillment, and wholeness in us already. Our job is to excavate it.

What should you do when a fellow soul mate has a flare-up? Nothing. It is not your problem...unless you buy into it. Just chalk it up to masculine PMS..."**P**ardon **M**y **S**oul"...and for goodness sake (literally), just pardon his soul. The golden rule is still in effect you know... *"Do unto others as you would have them do unto you."*

Soul Quest

I walked through life unresigned,
A restless agitation driving me.
I felt ideas inside so mystical,
So intense…that at times
I hesitated to blink for fear they would fade.
Irreversibly drawn to the inconceivable,
I was caught up in mediocrity of endless days.
Drowning…compromising…comatose…
Sabotaging…dying…ignoring self,
I could not…I would not accept the emptiness
As "Destination" in the heart of Father.
I knew…somewhere…someway…somehow
There would be a rendering off of impurities
And shadows…and clouds…that covered
My Visions…and Dreams…Myself.
The world inside beckoned,
I was endlessly scanning the horizon
Searching…demanding…insisting,
Destination unknown…and yet unrelenting.

Assignments

THE KINGDOM OF DEATH

So, did this kingdom step on your toes? Honesty is the only policy. If so, just ask for forgiveness…it's over just that quick.

1. **Years ago I heard, "The acid test of true Christianity is asking yourself: Are you fun to live with?"** So, are you fun to life with? Answer honestly in your journal. You could ask your nearest and dearest for the answer to that question…but you no doubt already know.

2. **In your time with Father** this week, sincerely ask Him to do for you, what David asked Him to do in Psalm 139: *"Search me [thoroughly], O God, and know my heart! Try me and know my thoughts! See if there is any wicked or hurtful way in me, and lead me in the way everlasting"* (emphasis added).

3. **Continue your morning pages. Have you discovered the *page–and–a–half secret* yet?** Many of us who are dedicated *morning-pages* addicts have discovered that the first page and a half of the three pages are just "stuff" we need to get out of the way and out of our mind before we start the day. The second half is the "good stuff" from a soul set free and sometimes straight from Father's heart delivered with clarity from our spirits. And as one of my favorite minister's says, *"One word from God can change your life forever."*

The Kingdom of Focus

A PLACE CALLED PEACE

I believe we are seeing in the distance the lights of *home*. Our eyes are searching the horizon for some long-ago, eternities-past landmarks—landmarks laid out by Father when we were conceived in the womb of His heart. The landmarks of *wholeness* and *peace*. The landmarks of *dreams* and *visions*. Many of us have been homesick for so many years, we hesitate to believe, that we are in truth, almost there.

Hesitate no longer, Little One; *home* is waiting; and Father has spread a table for you. It is full of everything He knows you enjoy. On a perfectly laid expanse of purest white linen, there are place settings of translucent white, gold-trimmed china resting on golden chargers. The rainbow prisms of the crystal glasses dance in the reflection of elegant candles held aloft in golden candelabras. And the flowers! Oh the flowers are everywhere...all your favorite colors—snowy white lilies and deep burgundy velvet roses. The color of palest pink blushes the silken surface of an orchid, and over there are violets sweet with the dew of a *new morning*. Father has waited for this day all your life...and now it's here. You are back in the *heart dream of God* where you began.

The trip may have been terribly hard at times, but you had what it took to get through. (After all, you are your Father's daughter.) You took on the frontier of your soul, faced down dragons breathing the black fire of fear, and held on to hope when all hope was gone. Forgiveness was a quality decision you made in the midst of undreamed-of devastation. You learned to read danger signs and found out that you cannot give satan an inch. And now when he comes, *he finds no place in you.*

Along the *journey*, you met the remarkable *lady* you are. Through diligence, you found out that *lady* can possess *peace* and be *centered* in the midst of a soul storm brought on by other people's unresolved issues. You learned that she has no need to straighten other people out, or to fear she is going to be taken advantage of, hurt, or wounded. In fact, she has no fear. Period. Father has promised her amazing and lovely things, and she knows Father intimately...*Up Close and Personal*...and Father cannot lie.

Father's promises to her, fills her soul with a fullness she did not know possible. Father has become her *Partner*, her *Friend*, her *Source*, her *Beginning*, and her *End*. He is her *Beloved*.

When she first began to read His love letters to her, they seemed unreal. She once gathered His sweet Words on a page one after another like perfect pearls on a silver thread. Because she was so unused to loving Words, she read them over and over. Then after a while, there were too many of them, and she placed them in a treasure box where they continue to dance through her soul leaving an iridescent glow on her life. She took the silver thread, tied her heart to His, and there she lives.

Welcome home, Little One...Father's heart has missed you.

A Soul Surrenders to Love

Have you found her yet? You will. She is the ideal. She is your goal. She is the real *YOU*. She is part one of the *golden dream in the heart of God* for you. It may take you a while to recognize her. But you will. Not only will you recognize her, but the people around you will know something has changed. Perhaps they will see her before the mirror tells you she is here. Cinderella has gone to the ball. She has met her *Prince*, and life will never be the same. She may, for a short time, still be dressed in her apron sweeping the ashes off the hearth; but even the apron is worn with a new dignity. The tranquility they see in the windows of her soul is unmistakable. She is *royalty*, and she is beginning to know it.

Even as she goes about her daily life, she is slipping away every once in a while to confer with her *royal Father* about her future. He is training her to be a *princess in the realm of glory*. He is training her in the *family business* of touching lives with *love* and imparting *peace*. He is continuing to give her instruction, and promises, and hope.

Sing My child, you who tried so hard and lost so much. For your time has come and you are now giving birth to many, many dreams. Enlarge your vision...stretch out and inhabit a larger place: spare not; lengthen your cords and strengthen your stakes, for you will spread abroad to the right hand and to the left and your new dreams will fill the desolate places in your yesterdays. Fear not, your days of sadness are over...don't be confounded...or depressed. You will never again be put to shame. You shall completely forget the shame of your past and you will not seriously remember the reproach of being alone. For I am your Maker...I am the one who takes care of you. The Lord of Hosts is My name...the Holy One is your Redeemer...I Am God of the whole earth. I called you when you were a woman forsaken, grieved in spirit, and heart sore...even as one who was chosen and then rejected and scorned. It may seem as if I had rejected you, but with great compassion and mercy I have gathered you to Me. My face was hidden for a brief moment, but with age-enduring love I have sought you out. My goodness and kindness and mercy have been searching for you. For this is like the days of Noah to Me, when I gave Noah the covenant rainbow as a sign that I would never cover the earth with water again. I Am promising you, Little One...in fact I swear to you, My child, I will never be angry at you or rebuke you. Even if the mountains depart and the hills be shaken and removed, yet My love and kindness shall not depart from you, nor will I remove My covenant of peace and completeness...for I have compassion on you. I know you were afflicted, storm-tossed and not comforted... but look at what I am going to do! I am about to set your days in fair colors and in such a way to enhance their brilliance...and your new foundations, My child, will be laid with the blue sapphires of royalty. I will make the windows of your soul sparkle with joy, and all your walls will be built by Me and be precious in My sight. I will take care of your children and I will teach them and they will be obedient to My will for their individual lives. Great will be the peace and undisturbed composure of your children. You will establish yourself in right standing with

Me, in accordance with My plan and purpose for your life. You will be far away from even the thought of oppression or destruction, for you shall not fear. Because you don't fear...oppression and destruction and terror...it can't come near you. Look, someone in your life may try to stir up strife, but it is not from Me. Whoever comes against you shall fall. His plans as dust around your feet. I created the enemy of your soul...but no weapon he forms against you can possibly prosper and every tongue that shall rise against you in judgment **you** *shall show to be in the wrong. I give you peace, righteousness, security, triumph over opposition...this is your heritage as My child. As My image is reproduced in your soul, you will obtain righteousness and vindication...this is that which I impart to you* (Isaiah 54, paraphrased from the Amplified Bible, *Up Close and Personal*).

Protecting Our Position

Whether *the lady* is a full visual reality, or you get glimpses of her only now and then, the position she holds and the territory she has taken on this *journey* must be protected. The dragons are still breathing fire, satan is still trying to deceive, and snipers may yet be hiding in their soul-built boxes. Not only that, but because of where we have been, our excitement about the revelations we have received, and the love we have for the people around us, we may be in danger of "wet blankets."

You know the "wet blankets"—like the negative friend, pastor, husband, child, parent, or sibling who wants to conjure up our second, third, and fourth thoughts for us—the ones who give us their opinion, free advice, or the unsought-after benefit of their experience.

"Ohhhh, those wet blankets!"

Yeah...those are the ones. The ones who say, "Just wondered if you had thought of this..." as they, "for our own good," lay a well-placed doubt on the brightness of our flame. They are the ones who "for our own good" tell us 15 things wrong with the article, poem, or book before they ever say something positive. If this sounds like "experience" talking here...you're right. Beware! Beware!

Women love to talk, have others share their dreams, and be validated in their endeavors—and therein lies a problem. We want so desperately to share the awesome things Father is imparting into our spirits, that history is forgotten, wisdom is thrown to the wind, and we reach for our nearest wet blanket. We blurt out to our nearest-and-dearest, most skeptical loved one what Father has said on the *morning pages*...the business He has dropped into our heart...the marketing plan He is unfolding...the key we know to be the answer to our financial future...the revelation about the *call of God* on our life. And then true to form, they try to turn down the flame of our newly lit candle...or put it out altogether.

It's not that they want to be wet blankets; usually they have our best interest at heart. They may even have a lot of expertise and worldly wisdom. But *unless* they are themselves moving from a center of positive core beliefs, they have almost nothing to add to the *wisdom of the plan* Father has for us. Because they are so practiced at seeing in the natural, their spiritual vision is seriously impaired. We must never forget that Father's ways are *"past finding out,"* unless of course, you have been in the *Throne Room* looking *Up Close and Personal* at the map.

Many a Christian wife, married to a Christian man whose soul has not been renewed, looks almost desperately for a way to connect with her husband. She wants them as a couple to have communication, to talk together, make plans to serve God together...just anything together.

So when she gets a revelation, an insight, an idea she knows is from God, she almost runs to her man to share. The problem is, her man can't see past his own history of negative cores. He hasn't been *practicing the presence,* reading the *Word,* or abiding in the *secret place.* All he has been doing is exactly what he has always done...which is why he is in the shape he's in. Our tendency to grab our wet blanket to wrap around our *dream, vision,* or *new beginning* makes about as much sense as sterilizing a needle that is going to be used for a lethal injection. No sense at all.

The remedy? Set boundaries around everything Father is doing in your life. Don't allow anyone else to take away the time you spend in the *presence.* Don't share your *morning pages* with just anybody. Keep your own counsel. Move silently among doubters. Practice self-containment. Voice your new freedom only to kindred souls, and choose those souls wisely. List the people who will understand. List the ones who can't possibly know where you are coming from at this point in their lives. Name your W.B.'s for what they are…wet blankets. Wrap yourself in something else—like the arms of Father, like the Word, like the *peace* you are finding inside *the lady*. Wrap yourself in *wisdom*.

Wisdom Is the Principle Thing

At our Ministry Center every Thursday evening, my husband teaches School of Wisdom. The foundation verse for these teachings is Proverbs 4:7: *The beginning of Wisdom is: get wisdom (skillful and godly Wisdom)! [For skillful and godly Wisdom is the principle thing].* Paraphrased *Up Close and Personal it says, "The very most important thing you can ever get, without exception, Is wisdom."*

The whole Book of Proverbs deals with this vital subject. Among other results of wisdom are the ones listed in Proverbs 4:

Wisdom will…

• Keep, defend, and protect you.

• Guard you if you love her.

• Exalt and promote you.

• Bring you to honor when you embrace her.

• Give to your head a wreath of gracefulness.

• Deliver a crown of beauty and glory to you.

• Enable you to live longer if you embrace her.

• Help you to understand the ways and purposes of God.

• Ensure that when you walk, your steps will not be hampered.

• Make your path clear and open…when you run you will never stumble.

Is it no wonder that Solomon admonishes us in verse 13 to *"take firm hold of instruction (wisdom), do not let go; guard her, for she is your life."*

If that wasn't enough, take a look at Proverbs 8:17-21:

I [Wisdom] love those who love me, and those who seek me early and diligently shall find me. Riches and honor are with me, enduring wealth and righteousness (uprightness in every area and relation, and right standing with God). My fruit is better than gold, yes, than refined gold, and my increase than choice silver. I (Wisdom) walk in the way of righteousness (moral and spiritual rectitude in every area and relation), in the midst of the paths of justice, that I may cause those who love me to inherit [true] riches and that I may fill their treasuries.

The *wisdom of God* is our focus. It is our only focus. It is why this book was written. As you can see from the few verses shared above, if we have the *wisdom of God*, it adds to our life all things. It all adds up to *peace*…nothing missing and nothing broken. Now that we know what has hindered us, and have removed the hindrances out of our souls, and have experienced healing, we can begin to expect the *wisdom of God* to flow in our lives, helping us to create *days of Heaven on earth*.

Centered

We must practice and stay *centered*. We have no option. We must know our *place*. If we do not know where we stand within ourselves, where does that leave us? When we stand centered in our own place in Him, it will become clear what our choices are and which ones to make. We have to continue to stand in our own place and know we are there.

Now that we know our *destiny, call,* and *assignment* are in the heart of God, and the wisdom to connect to His heart is in the *Word*, in the *presence*, and in our being *centered* in Him, all we have to do is…do it. Spend time in the *Word*…time in His *presence*…time in *centering* (listening for the still small voice in our spirits, becoming so sensitive to Him that His slightest breath will be discernible to you).

Don't tell me you don't have time. We have traveled this *journey* together for too long for me to listen to excuses. We went through the *kingdom of excuses* a few weeks back. We know how easy it is to bail out on ourselves. We know each other too well by now to play games, religious or otherwise. We are friends…friends are honest with each other. So, Girlfriend, I'm telling you, "Time is relative…and we're running out of it"—at least the earth kind of time. Jesus is coming back soon for a *glorious Church* without spot or wrinkle. We are the *signs and wonders* generation. My guess is you, like me, have barely begun to live *your best life, your call, your passion, your assignment*.

Our time is *now*. Father has *now "spread the table before us in the presence of our enemies"*—*now*—not when we get to Heaven; we will have no enemies in Heaven. Here and *now*, we are to walk upon the earth as *princesses*, full of the grace and power that is our rightful inheritance. Our time is *now*. And considering all we have at stake, any price we have to pay—time, discipline, reproach from loved ones, less TV, dying to self, getting up earlier, whatever—is a small price for all we have to gain.

Proven Fact Number One: *We find time for every single thing that is important to us (every single thing).*

Proven Fact Number Two: *We Christians spend hours waiting in line to hear a special speaker, or to get into a sports event, and we spend many more hours watching mindless television.*

To discover our assignment, we must spend some *quality* time being with Father and renewing our mind with the Word.

P.S. Jesus went apart from His very busy life to spend time with Father...that was the secret of His success.

Five More Questions

Are we through bailing out on our own future?

Are we willing to sell all we have, to own a pearl of great price?

What is it worth to live in His presence 24/7?

Are we ready to take over our part in the family business?

What price are we willing to pay for the gaining of our soul?

Someplace in Time

Someplace in time
My life was planned
In precise detail
And poetic beauty.
Spirit Father knew me
And called my name
Someplace in time

Someplace in time
All the elements
Of the universe
Got ready to rush
To my aid
When Spirit Father
Called my name.

So here I am and
My place in time
Is now.

Assignments

THE KINGDOM OF FOCUS

1. **Record in your journal five *life-altering* concepts you have discovered on this journey.**

2. **Record what you intend to do with the information you now own.** Remember *information* alone will not bring change, but a *quality decision* to put into practice said information, day after day, will change everything.

3. **Your time in *His presence*** ought to be at least one hour a day by now…30 minutes on the *morning pages*…30 minutes just with Him.

4. **Go back and read your *morning pages*.** Take a marker and highlight the parts that you feel came from Him, through your spirit via your renewed soul. This will take some practice, but He is there to help you.

5. **Draw a large circle in your journal.** Inside the circle write a *dream* that Father has placed in your heart. It may be a business, a book to write, a ministry, a work of art, a school you want to go to, a job you want to have, a new career, a nice home, a godly mate, a daddy for your fatherless children—whatever is the desire of your heart. Outside the circle, write the names of suspected "wet blankets." You know who they are; if you're not sure, ask. The Holy Spirit is there *"to lead you into all truth."* If you feel a "caution," like a yellow light flashing, in your inner man (spirit), pay attention

and proceed carefully. Inside the circle write the name or names of people you know who are not in the "Wet Blanket Ministry"—a kindred soul—and share the dream. Wrap yourself and your *dream* in *peace* and in the *Word*. **Don't reach for your wet blanket.**

A Word to the Wise

Do not tolerate anyone who tries to throw cold water on your newly lighted candle. Forget good intentions. Forget they didn't mean it. Set your focus and set your boundaries.

Timing Is Everything

The time to share with your nearest and dearest resident wet blanket is when the *dream* has manifested the resources to carry itself out. "Faith is the substance of the things hoped for." **When you hold the "substance" or title deed in your hand...tell the world!**

Don't worry, it will manifest.

When Father designed your specific dream, the golden one in His heart, He set aside every single resource you will ever need to fulfill that dream in the most excellent way. When the time arrives for your specific call, destiny, assignment to manifest, you will have in your hand, in reality, everything you will need at the absolutely perfect time. He will not be one second late...not one penny short. That is the time to tell the wet blankets in your life—not before.

Welcome Home

❧

We have just stepped into *peace*. It's been a long trip, but there's the gate to the *Peaceful Kingdom* where nothing is missing and nothing is broken. There it is—"The Place" where we discover and walk out our personal *assignment*, the *golden dream in the heart of God* uniquely designed for us.

One thing is for sure…if you have used the travel map laid out in this book, a number of things are different. You are, or well on your way to being, a different woman than the fragmented soul that began this *journey*. You know the truth about many things, and the truth that you know has set you free.

You *know* where and how satan has been able to steal from you in the past. You *know* Father better. You *know* how to make the Word *Up Close and Personal*. You *know* how unique and special you are in the eyes of Father. Through the *morning pages* you have learned how to put your ear down to your soul and listen real hard.

There is a certain calmness in your soul. You have learned to live in the moment by becoming *centered* in Him. Words like *peace, quietness, joy, knowing, clarity* have new meanings for you. Words like *snipers, wet blankets,* and *PMS* (**P**ardon **M**y **S**oul) also have new meanings. Most of the time, you have chosen "strategic disassociate" when you have run upon someone else's soul issues. In other words, you have learned to dwell in the *secret place* inside yourself and get the view from Heaven's perspective.

You see things differently. You see people differently. You see life differently. *You*, your spirit is gaining ascendancy over your soul, and for that matter, your body as well. Along the path you have lightened your load, and at the same time you have picked up a few treasures to take into your new life. As we get our souls into position to flow in the *call of God* upon our lives, an interesting thing happens. Not only does our mind, will, and emotions change, as baggage, soul issues, and negative core beliefs are exposed and confronted; but other things are changing as well.

It has been said that "change is getting rid of the past to make room for the future"; this is true in all areas of our lives. In the years as I have had the honor of traveling on this *journey* with other *pioneers*, I have consistently seen an interesting result of spiritual-soul growth.

Over the months of purging the "junk" out of your soul, you no doubt, have experienced the urge to get rid of other "stuff' in your life." You find yourself also cleaning out hidden areas of your home. Closets, drawers, and cupboards all come under the exacting eye of the fresh, new perspective of your soul. You open a cabinet one day and it hits you, "Order...I must have order!"...and you ruthlessly throw out 27 plastic butter tubs, the chipped china, and all the holey dish towels.

You clean the closets, blessing Goodwill with all the "Why-on-earth-did-I-buy-that?" items. By now you probably know you "bought that" because it was cheap (sale rack mentality), or you were trying to fill a space in your needy soul. Whatever the case, these things are not the "real you," and now you know it.

One woman on the *journey* woke up to this fact one day after she had gotten dressed and gone to work. She had put on a heretofore favorite outfit. She had worn it many times, but as she passed a mirror on that fateful day, she stopped and really looked at herself with eyes that really see. Her reaction? "That's not who I am!" She went home and put the whole outfit in the trash.

When she shared this with me a few weeks after the incident, I recalled that she "happened" to come by the Ministry Center that day. I remember looking at her and getting the impression, "That outfit is not Gracie."

That's who Gracie used to be. The new Gracie had a different style...and so do you. Colors, clothes, food, relationships, daily habits, shopping habits, hairstyle, and any other number of other things are subject to change as you excavate your authentic self.

What Happened?

What happened is we are proving the theory that we create our lives from the inside out. Our souls, being the creative center of our spirits (us), will create around us what is going on within us. As our mind is being renewed, excess baggage is dropped, and negative core beliefs are exposed and reprogrammed by the Word of God into positive core beliefs; this allows good orderly direction to issue from our souls into our daily lives. Order in...order out.

We have, in essence, cleaned out the hidden clutter of our souls; therefore, the Holy Spirit residing in our human spirit has now gained ascendancy. We can hear "The Voice" though it may be still and small; but because our souls have shut up their continuous clamoring of opinions, we now hear Him loud and clear.

Some days we may not know exactly who we are anymore; so much had changed. Sometimes our self-assurance can be a little hard to swallow for our family and friends. While I had to admire her honesty, I can't say I recommend what one woman on the *journey* did. She left this message on her answering machine: "Thank you for calling; I am out just now. I appreciate the fact that you cared enough to call me. Please leave a name and number. I am making some changes in my life right now, and if I don't return your call...you are one of them."

So once again, "Welcome Home." You are about to get in touch with your family tree and find in its roots your *call, destiny, assignment*. You are now replanted in the fertile field of the "homeland" (the heart of God). The blood of Jesus and the Word have washed all the toxins out of the soul of your spirit. As you continue to do as Spirit leads, practice all you have learned on our *journey*, and rest in the sunshine of His love, your roots will go deeper and deeper. And you, Little One, beloved of God, will grow to be a mighty tree, and under your branches many shall find *peace*.

Epilogue

———————— ❧ ————————

Thank you for sharing the *journey*. There has been more than one wake-up moment along the way. I can honestly say that the months I have put this together have been the most amazing time of growth for me and my "beloved enablers/sounding boards." Time after time, I would sit down at my computer to write and be amazed at what was going onto the screen. I would quickly print it and take it to my beloveds and say, "Read this! Look what Father is saying!" I pray it will impact your life in the same incredible way it has impacted us.

The Search for Peace was never meant to be a solitary *journey*. Please share this with others; the concepts work for men as well as women, for the young as well as the older. Our local group of *Women of Peace* has an age span from 13 to late 70's. No one is ever too young or too old to find their personal *dream in the heart of God*. Father has a wonderful plan for your life, and the details are inside you, waiting to be discovered.

So until next time, may the *God of peace* fill your life with all good things and sanctify you completely—*spirit, soul, and body*.

Postscript: Father wishes above all things that you prosper and be in health, just as your soul prospers. And Girlfriend…that's just the way it works. When your soul prospers, everything around you prospers. Enjoy!

- The Beginning -

Questions and Answers on the Journey

Just for the Record

Over the years that I have taught from this material, I have been asked a number of questions. The questions differ depending on which part of the Body of Christ is doing the asking...here are a few of them. I hope they help clarify any foggy places you may have encountered on your *Search for Peace.*

- **Question:** The assignments and the morning pages seem like they will take a lot of time. I am already so busy I don't know what to do. How do I find the time?

- **Answer:** Good question. The thing I have discovered from experience, and I might add, a number of other very busy women have realized, is a cluttered soul is a big time waster. It flies from one project to another never really accomplishing much of anything of lasting importance. A soul is a lover of activity; we must control its tendencies to be too busy.

  It's sort of like the Mary and Martha thing. The story is found in chapter 10 of the Book of Luke. Martha is very much like our unrenewed soul—"*...anxious and troubled about many things.*" But Scripture says that "*there is only need of one thing...*" and Mary, who represents our born-again spirits, anxious to hear the voice of God, "*chose the good portion (that which is to her advantage)....*"

It all boils down to what we choose. We can make a quality decision to go after *more*...or a decision to continue to tolerate the way things are now.

What We Choose to Tolerate Will Never Change.

Most importantly, we must remember that Father wants us free more than we want to be free. We might want wholeness because we are tired of being broken. He wants us whole so He can fulfill His dream for us, which is far beyond just getting fixed. By now we ought to know that when Father wants something done, Father will find a way to get it done. All He needs is our cooperation. He knows every detail of you and your life, like the back of His hand. Just ask Him about the time. He will give wonderful creative ideas to any daughter who requests His help about time management.

Time is no problem to Father; He has plenty of it. And so do we *if we only do* what is needful. In all your life, nothing is more important than renewing your mind with the Word of God. That one *needful* thing will literally transform every single part of your life. When this fact becomes a reality, you will set boundaries around your time with Father, around your time in the Word, around your time doing the assignments. Remember, a soul set free is a sign and a wonder...and *that* is our destination.

Postscript: In the Twenty-third Psalm David wrote, "*He restores my soul.*" So just do whatever it takes to let Him restore your soul. It will be worth the effort.

- **Question:** What part does demonic spirits play in our ongoing problems?

- **Answer:** A lot...but only because we have given them place. A whole woman, healed from past wounds, and walking 24/7 in the very presence of God is not a candidate for abuse from man or satan.

- **Question:** What about deliverance ministries? Can they help us get free from some of the problems in our souls?

- **Answer:** Deliverance, or the casting out of demons, is a valid New Testament ministry. But care must be taken that, after the demon is cast out, whatever "door" he came in is now closed to him. Usually these doors are unmet needs, unhealed hurts, or unresolved issues located in our souls. A demon cannot just decide to move in on your soul and proceed to steal your peace. A soul-harassing demon must have a point of entrance. Remember the story that Jesus related in Matthew 12:43-45:

When the unclean spirit has gone out of a man [woman], it roams through dry [arid] places in search of rest, but it does not find any. Then it says, I will go back to my house from which I came out. And when it arrives, it finds the place unoccupied, swept, put in order, and decorated. Then it goes and brings with it seven other spirits more wicked than itself, and they go in and make their home there. And the last condition of that man [woman] becomes worse than the first.

If deliverance takes place, make absolutely sure that the empty space is filled with the **Word of God**. A soul will be filled with something. If it is cleaned out and filled with the Word, satan can find no place, even if he sends seven more demons worse than the first. **Remember, satan is not who defeats us; it is his access to us that defeats us.**

- **Question:** Morning pages sound a little bit strange. Do they work for everybody?

- **Answer:** I have never met or heard of anyone who did not benefit from morning pages. Almost everybody goes into this exercise dubious. The ones who stick with it reap an abundance of insight into themselves. There are people who 10 years. They would never think of giving them up.

Some of the dyed-in-the-wool devotees are not even Christians. Lawyers say getting all the early morning clutter out of their heads helps them argue their cases better in court. Dancers say it improves their balance. Writers say it unblocks them. (I have found that one to be the truth.) Doctors have found the answer to a patient's puzzling illness flowing out on the pages. Runners say the consistent practice improves their timing.

Almost everybody says the pages have helped them be more productive in all areas of their lives. Yes, they seem to work for everybody, and everything works better for a Christian.

My favorite part of the morning pages is when my soul gets out of the way and I find Father talking to me...telling me things *Up Close and Personal.*

- **Question:** I finished the book and completed the twelve weeks of assignments...what now?

- **Answer:** Now, you *journey on.* Reread the book. Get a friend, or better yet, a group of friends and travel the journey together. Continue to read the Word, paraphrasing it *Up Close and Personal.* Write it in your journal. Continue your *morning pages*...give satan no place. Practice, practice, practice the *presence* all the time. *Practice His presence* even when you have to make small decisions...like what to order off a menu, what to fix for dinner, when you need to make a shopping decision.

Every decision is a holy moment moving you toward your *best self,* or away from it. Center in. He really is eager to lead and guide you. If we have a fully developed habit of *practicing His presence* in the small everyday things, then when satan raises his ugly head with what appears to be a big problem, our souls will automatically flee into *the presence* to receive guidance. Practice creates habits.

So until the second book in this series is published, write or E-mail us for information about forthcoming meetings, or to inquire about setting up a meeting, retreat, or workshop in your area.

And last, but not least, practice Second Timothy 2:2:

And the [instructions] which you have learned from me, along with many witnesses, transmit, teach, and entrust [as a deposit] to reliable and faithful women who will then be competent and qualified to teach others also (paraphrased from the Amplified Bible, *Up Close and Personal*).

Peace in Him,

Wanda

Ministry Contact Information

Wanda would like to hear from you.
To set up workshops, retreats, or meetings,
or just to share your personal journey,

E-mail her at:
Thesearchforpeace.com
or
elshaddaiim@aol.com

Suggested Reading

To move you closer
to the *Golden Dream*
in *Father's Heart* for you.

WOMAN, THOU ART LOOSED!

Let your heart be warmed as the oil of T.D. Jakes' teaching flows from your mind to your spirit. The balm of this book will soothe all manner of traumas, tragedies, and disappointments. For the single parent and the battered wife, for the abused girl and the insecure woman, there is a cure for the crisis!

ISBN 1-7684-3040-2

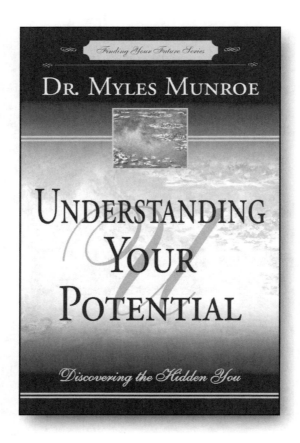

UNDERSTANDING YOUR POTENTIAL

This is a motivating, provocative look at the awesome potential trapped within you, waiting to be realized. This book will cause you to be uncomfortable with your present state of accomplishment and dissatisfied with resting on your past success.

ISBN 1-56043-046-X

Additional copies of this book and other
book titles from DESTINY IMAGE are
available at your local bookstore.

For a bookstore near you, call 1-800-722-6774.

Send a request for a catalog to:

Destiny Image® Publishers, Inc.

P.O. Box 310
Shippensburg, PA 17257-0310

*"Speaking to the Purposes of God for This
Generation and for the Generations to Come"*

For a complete list of our titles,
visit us at www.destinyimage.com